Praise for Charles Kenny's *Getting Better*..

"Provocative.... Our image of African stagnation is closely tied to our fixation with GDP, Kenny suggests, producing a highly distorted picture of reality."
    —*The Nation*

"Kenny offers a lighthearted critical survey of what economists have had to say about the determinants of economic growth, but he argues that growth, although important and desirable, should not be the main objective."
    —*Foreign Affairs*

"Original, unusual, and radical thinking."
    —Mark Bittman, *New York Times* Opinionator Blog

"The real question is not *whether* foreign aid and local government programs can work—it's which programs work and which do not. The most hopeful part of Mr. Kenny's hopeful message is that progress in health, education and human rights may ultimately bring economic progress as well."
    —David Leonhardt, Economic Scene, *New York Times*

"Kenny's book sheds an extremely underrated light on the positive aspects of global development and how the 21st century is ushering in the best of times in terms of health, education, political freedoms and access to infrastructure and new technologies, benefiting even the poorest in the world.... We love good news, and Kenny certainly delivers.... Be sure to check out Kenny's new book—it's a great read."
    —*One*

"An antidote to the pessimism many of us feel about the state of the world."
    —*Huffington Post*

D0596200

"[*Getting Better* is] persuasive and a very pleasant short book."
  —Matt Yglesias, Think Progress

"[A] tremendously bracing book."
  —*Choice*

"Gloom and doom have long been the default view of global poverty. It would take a clear-eyed and courageous researcher to show that the orthodox viewpoint is wrong. Such a researcher has finally appeared in Charles Kenny, who shows convincingly that most trends in human well-being worldwide, and region by region, are happily, dramatically positive. Read this delightful book and you will never look at global economic development the same way again."
  —William Easterly, Professor of Economics at New York University and author of *The White Man's Burden: Why the West's Efforts to Aid the Rest Have Done So Much Ill and So Little Good* and *The Elusive Quest for Growth: Economists' Adventures and Misadventures in the Tropics*

"*Getting Better* makes an important point. . . . Kenny employs a whole range of examples to illustrate these major empirical findings in ways that make the story quite enthralling."
  —Jeni Klugman, director and lead author of the United Nations Development Program's Human Development Report; *Foreign Policy* Book Club (online)

"Charles Kenny's terrific new book, *Getting Better*, covers a wide range of global development issues. . . . And Kenny makes a convincing case that the quality of life in poorer countries has improved greatly over the years—and will likely continue to improve—even if incomes in those countries remain stubbornly difficult to lift."
  —Bradford Plumer, associate editor of the *New Republic*; *Foreign Policy* Book Club (online)

"[A] fantastic new book. . . . In our bad-news-first world, these successes have received too little attention; let's hope that Kenny's book gives the pessimists pause."

> —Garett Jones, BB&T Professor at the Mercatus Center
> and Researcher at the Center for Study of Public Choice,
> George Mason University; *Foreign Policy* Book Club (online)

"[Kenny's] writing is good 'pop economics'—chatty, humorous and at times elegant. . . . He's also an ace killer fact merchant and a voracious trawler of research and stats—definitely a gold mine for time-starved development advocates. . . . An excellent run-through of the shifting (and frequently circular) tides of received wisdom on growth and development."

> —Duncan Greene, Oxfam International,
> From Poverty to Power Blog

"Charles Kenny . . . has written an excellent, factually informed, and sophisticated account of the changes in income and quality of life in development over recent decades in a fully engaging way."

> —Lant Pritchett, Harvard Kennedy School, *Population and Development Review*

"*Getting Better* is a wonderful book: a great read, a compelling argument, and what will be a controversial bottom line—that growth is not after all necessary for poverty reduction. In a surprising riposte to GDP-focused economists and aid skeptics, Charles Kenny brings readers not just Malthus, Arthur Lewis, Sen and Sachs, but Kipling, Tolstoy, and the unfortunate Mungo Park. Here is a thoughtful and sweeping take on what we don't know about why countries grow and what we do know about how ideas and technology and yes aid are improving lives everywhere."

> —Nancy Birdsall, President of the Center for
> Global Development

"Charles Kenny is one of the best and deepest writers on economic growth and its relationship to quality of life in the modern world. This book represents the pinnacle of his thought."
 —Tyler Cowen, Holbert C. Harris Professor of Economics, George Mason University

"This nuanced and brilliant book is a must-read for anybody who wants to understand the complexity of development. Kenny doesn't traffic in trite or facile diagnoses or solutions; instead, he compellingly lays out both the obstacles to success and the good reasons to be hopeful. I learned more from this book than from any other book I've ever read: it's chock-full of important facts, corralled masterfully. Enjoy, and be illuminated!"
 —Felix Salmon, finance blogger for *Reuters*

"The novelty of Kenny's book is its factual character. All his arguments are backed by facts about the development experience of different countries. This gives the book a certain liveliness which you rarely find in works about economic development."
 —EH.net

"*Getting Better* is . . . a refreshing departure from the current pessimism with respect to global development. . . . [*Getting Better* has a] powerful message that the future is bright. In the midst of negativity, Charles Kenny's *Getting Better* provides a bold and refreshing vision for how we can build on existing substantial progress."
 —*The Business Economist* (London)

"Kenny is hardly sanguine in his view of developmental progress, nor unrealistic about the challenges that the majority world still faces, but he wants the massive quality of life improvements that have already taken place to be fully acknowledged . . . so that they can, in turn, spur further progress."
 —*African Business*

"Let Charles Kenny take you on a historical bird's-eye view: it'll do you good. . . . This is an immensely useful book because it forces readers to focus on the things that really matter, on the major trends. [Kenny] draws a compelling and uplifting picture of progress across the globe, neatly packaged in a small, highly readable book."

—*Enterprise Development & Microfinance*

"Charles Kenny . . . one of the most thoughtful people writing on development these days, has produced a fascinating and informative book. . . . *Getting Better* is a counterweight to the growing cadre of development assistance naysayers. . . . Kenny has done the international aid community a great service by reminding us that there is more to development than 'income' and that our report card in these other areas is good."

—Dennis de Tray, Results for Development Institute

"Charles Kenny's *Getting Better* is a refreshing departure from the current pessimism and offers a more grounded perspective on global development. . . . In the midst of negativity, Charles Kenny's *Getting Better* provides a bold and refreshing vision for how we can build on existing substantial progress."

—*Zambian Economist*

"Everyone knows that bad news is news, while the story line that things are spinning along just as they should is generally met with a resounding yawn. . . . Kenny's new book, *Getting Better*, . . . will provide an attitude adjustment."

—Laura Freschi, Associate Director, NYU Development Research Institute / AidWatch Blog

"*Getting Better* is one excellent antidote to development pessimism. At the centre of Kenny's argument is the claim that . . . dramatic progress has still taken place almost everywhere on Earth."

—*Development Policy Blog* (Australian National University)

"A nice contrast. . . . Kenny points to advances in education, health, human rights, and the continuing march of innovation and ideas to give comfort to optimists everywhere."
　　—*Time Out for Entertainment* (Denver)

"Amusing . . . mischievous . . . forceful . . . *Getting Better* ends with a call for 'realistic optimism.'"
　　—*The Enlightened Economist*

"A fine survey recommended for any social issues collection."
　　—*Midwest Book Review: California Bookwatch*

"A World Bank economist's insightful examination of the effectiveness of global development. . . . Relying on a relaxed approach flecked with sarcasm and wit, Kenny's accessible and generally jargon-free prose easily guides readers through the contentious and political aspects of global development and the ideologies competing to control it. A poignant and optimistic rebuttal to critics of global development."
　　—*Kirkus Reviews*

GETTING
BETTER

GETTING

BETTER

Why Global Development Is Succeeding—
And How We Can Improve the
World Even More

Charles Kenny

BASIC BOOKS

A MEMBER OF THE PERSEUS BOOKS GROUP

New York

Copyright © 2011 by Charles Kenny
Foreword copyright © 2012 by Bill Gates
Hardcover first published in 2011 by Basic Books,
A Member of the Perseus Books Group
Paperback first published in 2012 by Basic Books

All rights reserved.
No part of this book may be reproduced in any manner
whatsoever without written permission except in the case of
brief quotations embodied in critical articles and reviews. For
information, address Basic Books, 250 West 57th Street, 15th
Floor, New York, NY 10107.

Books published by Basic Books are available at special
discounts for bulk purchases in the United States by
corporations, institutions, and other organizations. For more
information, please contact the Special Markets Department at
the Perseus Books Group, 2300 Chestnut Street, Suite 200,
Philadelphia, PA 19103, or call (800) 810-4145, ext. 5000, or
e-mail special.markets@perseusbooks.com.

The Library of Congress has catalogued the hardcover as follows:
Kenny, Charles.
  Getting better : why global development is succeeding : and
how we can improve the world even more / Charles Kenny.
    p. cm.
  Includes bibliographical references and index.
  ISBN 978-0-465-02015-7 (alk. paper)
  1. Economic development. 2. Quality of life. I. Title.
  HD75.K46 2011
  306—dc22
                                                    2010037680

E-book ISBN: 978-0-465-02050-8
Paperback ISBN: 978-0-465-03103-0
Revised e-book ISBN: 978-0-465-03288-4

To Alex and Julia

CONTENTS

FOREWORD TO THE
PAPERBACK EDITION

....

Bill Gates

With the global economy as turbulent as it has been lately, pessimism is popular, and short-term thinking is too. So, stepping into the public square to announce that foreign aid is important and effective can be lonely work.

But fortunately, Charles Kenny has done just that. *Getting Better* sheds light on the importance and effectiveness of foreign aid as a powerful tool to build broader global quality of life. Kenny shows that aid money can and does work. It improves people's lives and makes the world a better and safer place.

Getting Better dispels the gloom and doom with a wealth of convincing data on the remarkable, underappreciated progress that almost all developing countries have achieved over the past several decades—many with the help of considerable aid support.

At less than 2 percent of public spending in most donor countries, aid's true impact has been obscured by a paradox. The billions of dollars that the West has poured into poor countries have had a limited impact on income, which is what most economists use to measure progress in living standards. Many countries in Africa today have real per-capita incomes lower than that of Britain at the time of the Roman Empire. Over the past several decades, through good times and bad, the income gap between rich and poor countries has grown. And no one really knows why.

But income is only one measure of success, and maybe not the most meaningful one. We care about it mostly as a proxy for what money can buy: food, shelter, health, education, security, and other factors that contribute to human well-being. More so than income, these are the things that development aid directly addresses. And by these measures—this is Mr. Kenny's great insight—quality of life, even in the world's poorest countries, has improved dramatically over the past several decades, far more than most people realize.

Fifty years ago, more than half the world's population struggled with getting enough daily calories. By the 1990s, this figure was below 10 percent. Famine affected less than three-tenths of 1 percent of the population in sub-Saharan Africa from 1990 to 2005. As Mr. Kenny suggests, the record has thoroughly disproved Malthusian prophecies of food shortages caused by spiraling population growth. Family sizes have fallen for many decades now in every region, including Africa.

And there's more good news. Virtually everywhere, infant mortality is down and life expectancy is up. In Africa, life expectancy has increased by ten years since 1960, despite the continent's HIV pandemic. Nearly 90 percent of the world's children are now enrolled in primary schools, compared with less than half in 1950. Literacy rates in the sub-Saharan region have more than doubled since 1970. Political and civil rights also have gained ground.

With reams of solid data to support his case, Mr. Kenny argues that governments and aid agencies have played important roles in this progress. He also recognizes that inevitably some development aid projects are wasteful and corrupt. Clearly, this should never be tolerated. But overall, when you look at the big picture, good things are happening—and aid has played a vital part.

And *Getting Better* has good suggestions for ways to make aid more efficient and effective. The spread of new technologies and ideas means that many of the best things in life are surprisingly cheap. Eradicating smallpox from the face of the earth, for example, cost about thirty-two cents per person in infected countries. In just six years, a drive to vaccinate African children against measles reduced the number who died of the disease by three-quarters, from more than five hundred thousand a year. Even larger gains in public health can still be achieved at a stunningly low cost relative to the benefits. Of the ten million children who die each year in poor countries, one-third could be saved through the wider use of breast-feeding, insecticide-treated bed nets, and oral rehydration therapy (a simple sugar and salt solution) to combat the effects of diarrhea.

After years of pessimism on the subject of foreign aid, Mr. Kenny's factual and thoughtful contribution is refreshing and much needed. He shines a light on the real successes of aid and the benefits that additional smart investment can bring. I hope that *Getting Better* will help strengthen our collective resolve to build a healthier and more productive future for all.

Bill Gates is the cofounder and chairman of Microsoft and cochair of the Bill & Melinda Gates Foundation.

PROLOGUE

An infant wakes up in an African village and whimpers for the breast. His mother reaches through the mosquito netting and lifts him onto her chest. He is slightly feverish from the injections he had the day before—still, better that than a case of measles. His elder sister runs in after a visit to the pit latrine, singing her ABCs as she washes her hands. She gobbles down some corn meal porridge while her mother pours water from the disinfectant jug. The little girl, already dressed in her school uniform, puts on her shoes, grabs her pen and exercise book, and trips off down the gravel road to school, leaving mother and baby with only the sounds of static and a radio announcer reading the news.

This is a wholly undramatic story—yet startling and beautiful in its own right. Similar tales of drama-free mornings are repeated countless times across the region every day. Nobody gets sick, nobody gets shot, and nobody dies. Kids go off to school, and parents to work. They return to food on the table and a peaceful night. Its beauty is in its banality, a sign of the considerable progress that African countries have made in extending a basic quality of life to ever more people. This book is about that progress in Africa and around the world, what has caused it, and how we can keep it going.

Despite counterclaims and hand wringing, things are getting better, everywhere. Rich countries may be getting richer faster than poor countries, and we may be unsure how to improve that situation, but poor countries and poor people aren't stuck in the nightmare of an ever-growing and unsupportable population, living on bare subsistence. Instead, those countries with the lowest quality of life are making the fastest progress in improving it—across a range of measures including health, education, and civil and political liberties. The progress is the result of the global spread of technologies and ideas—technologies like vaccinations, and ideas like "you should send your daughter to school." And Third World governments, alongside aid agencies and nonprofits, have played a vital role in extending the reach of these technologies and ideas.

All of this is not to deny continued deprivation and suffering worldwide, alongside considerable waste, incompetence, and corruption in government and assistance programs alike. But all of the progress that we have seen is a sign that things *can* get better, and that we have some considerable capacity to *make* them better. This, surely, is the best motivation to try even harder to overcome the deprivation and suffering that remains.

ONE

ABANDONING HOPE

··

I n 2009, the leaders of the world's largest economies congregated in London for their summit on the recent fiscal crisis. Following well-established precedent (international summits discussing global economic coordination and financial sector reform are more hackneyed than a Miss World pageant), the participants issued a declaration that included language on the need to sustain the progress of global development even in these tough economic times. "We start from the belief that prosperity is indivisible; that growth, to be sustained, has to be shared; and that our global plan for recovery must have at its heart the needs and jobs of hard-working families, not just in developed countries but in emerging markets and the poorest countries of the world too," suggested their final communiqué, which had largely been written before the world's leaders arrived in London. Much the same could have been said decades before, familiar to the attendees of the first "Global Economic Summit" of what would become the G-8, when it was held south of Paris in 1975 to discuss exchange rates and economic coordination in the midst of an oil crisis and, once again, global recession. Or, indeed, to the attendees of London's 1933 World Economic Conference, which greeted new US President Roosevelt in high hopes that he would reverse the regulatory trends of his predecessor in the midst of *that* global recession.

Outside the headquarters of the 2009 summit, 35,000 protesters also followed a familiar script, chanting in support of a kaleidoscope of causes—nuclear disarmament and an end to the Iraq war, action on climate change and banking reform. And many marched to protest the inability or unwillingness of their leaders to foster global development for the world's poorest inhabitants, as they had promised. These protesters saw the latest financial crisis as further evidence of the failure of economic development. In so doing, they, too, joined a historied chorus.

A host of others, from public intellectuals to the heads of international aid organizations to commentators and politicians on both the left and the right, shared the concerns of world leaders and protesters alike. In a widely accepted version of the recent history of global development, there are two things left to argue over—who is to blame, and what to do about it. But all agree about the current state of the planet: Much of the world is a cesspool of economic stagnation, overpopulation, malnutrition, ignorance, violence, and disease.

The Right would abandon "Third World rat-holes," as US Senator Jesse Helms once called them, to their inevitable fate. The Left looks at the same failure and blames continuing Western dominance—colonialism still rampant, but carried on in a different form as the neo-imperialism of the International Monetary Fund and the World Bank. Others argue that the problem lies with poor countries' geography and natural endowments, and blame the inadequacy of donor efforts to help overcome these barriers to progress. But in all interpretations, these "causes" are the root of the same blight—an abject failure to develop across much of the Third World, a crisis of global proportions.

"Crisis" might even be a generous way to refer to the performance of African countries over the forty or so years since independence, at least according to numerous commentators.
Robert Kaplan, in *The Ends of the Earth*, argues that Africa suf-
fers from "new age primitivism." Oxford University's Paul Collier
argues in his book *The Bottom Billion* that many African societies face a "fourteenth-century" reality of "civil war, plague, ignorance." Similarly, Harvard historian Niall Ferguson suggests
that "[e]mpires have their faults, no doubt. But independent
African governments have often been more exploitative and
worse for economic growth." Ferguson goes on to argue: "Africa's
problem is not a problem that aid can solve. On the contrary:
aid may simply make the problem worse."[1]

African economic stagnation is the big reason that Dambisa
Moyo (in her best seller *Dead Aid*) and Bill Easterly (in his, *The
White Man's Burden*) are skeptical about the role of aid, as well.
Gregory Clark, a professor of economics at the University of California at Davis, suggests of Africa: "[T]he whole technological
cornucopia of the last two hundred years [has] succeeded in producing among the lowest material living standards ever experienced. These African societies have remained trapped in the
Malthusian era." His resulting view of the efficacy of aid is suggested by the title of the book from which this quote is drawn:
A Farewell to Alms.[2]

Others, though, draw on exactly the same narrative of African
failure to call for a redoubling of aid efforts. Take Jeffrey Sachs,
Columbia University economist, special adviser to the United Nations secretary general, and one of the most widely cited development economists of the twenty-first century. He directs a program
designed to show the feasibility of meeting the United Nation's
Millennium Development Goals—an ambitious set of targets
for global progress in poverty reduction, improved health and

education, gender equality, and environmental sustainability—
by the target date of 2015. Sachs sees more aid to Africa as central to such an effort.

But the litany of failure—and in particular, African failure—
suggests that the success of development has been limited indeed.
And this, surely, is a significant indictment of the government
leaders, international agencies, nongovernment organizations,
and businesses that should have been fostering development. In
particular, it might suggest that those who despair of aid's impact
have a point. The last forty-two years have seen aid transfers to
developing countries worth approximately $2 trillion. That's
enough to bail out American International Group ten times or
so. If crisis is the only outcome, perhaps it's time to pack up the
aid missions and go home.

Luckily for the developing world—and for the leaders, organizations, and businesses involved—the reality of global progress
is something entirely different. While Africa and many other
parts of the planet have lagged in terms of income growth, they
have also seen historically unprecedented improvement in health
and education, gender equality, security, and human rights. And
much-maligned governments and aid agencies have played an
important role in that progress. Too narrow a focus on one indicator of success—income—has blinded many to these broader
advances, and that *is* a potential tragedy. Indeed, recognizing
this broader progress is an important first step in efforts to sustain it.

Before looking at that broader progress—and how we can make
the world even better—it's worth discussing what the "crisis of
development" is, and at what, in particular, Africa has failed. A
broad justification for a sense of failure regarding development

is based on evidence regarding income growth, which many economists and those who follow their analyses take as the ne plus ultra of how to measure economic progress. In truth, evidence on income growth is not encouraging. It suggests considerable long-term divergence in incomes between rich and poor countries worldwide, and a forty-year stagnation in African incomes that has left the average sub-Saharan country little richer than it was at independence. To take but one example, Senegal had an income per capita of $1,776 at independence in 1960 and of $1,407 in 2004. The United States, in contrast, had a GDP per capita a little more than seven times larger than Senegal in 1960. By 2004, the United States was around twenty-six times richer.

This divergence in incomes over the past fifty years, reflecting slower growth in poorer countries than in wealthy ones, spreads far beyond the Sahara. It is a worldwide phenomenon, brooking only limited exceptions, which are mostly concentrated in Asia. Consider Brazil, one of the bright spots in the South American economic scene. In 1975, Brazil's income per capita was 30 percent of the United States! By 2003, this had dropped to just above 20 percent.[3]

Evidence of a growing gap in global incomes—what Harvard economist Lant Pritchett calls "Divergence, Big Time"—fosters a broader sense of doom regarding development because income per capita has become the most common gauge for the overall quality of life in a country. We care about income because, worldwide, the answer to the question "Would you rather be richer or poorer" is pretty much always the same. As a character puts it in David Mamet's movie *Heist*, "Everybody needs money—that's why they call it *money*."[4]

Economists and noneconomists alike care about money because of overwhelming evidence that poorer people die younger, their children die more frequently, they lack access to education, they face higher rates of crime and violence. And while Western environmentalists may complain that more economic growth is unsustainable, and Western sociologists and psychologists may insist that there is little evidence it creates greater contentment, even these Cassandras are usually quiet on the subject of the importance of higher incomes in poor countries. Given all of that, rapid income growth is surely the holy grail of development.

From there, it is a simple step to the conclusion that, if income is diverging, so is the broad quality of life of citizens in different nations. And, in turn, that regions or countries on the wrong side of income divergence are failing at development. Based on income growth, much of the developing world's situation really does appear dire.

What is worse, we appear to have very little idea about which methods speed economic growth in poor countries. Take the East Asian Miracle of the last fifty years, for example. East Asia is the one region that has consistently upheld the promise of global *convergence* in income. A number of countries in that region grew significantly faster than the average for the club of rich countries that make up the Organization for Economic Cooperation and Development (OECD). GDP per capita growth rates averaged 6 percent in East Asia between 1975 and 2000, by far the best performance of any region in the world. These growth rates pulled hundreds of millions out of poverty and propelled a number of countries into high income status. South Korea, only as rich as Ghana in 1960, is now itself a member of the OECD, and Singapore is richer than Italy. This suggests the potential for rapid economic catch-up if only we could replicate the miracle.

If only.

As a result, the East Asian Miracle is a topic in numerous academic papers—over six thousand by one rough measure—and a subject of lively debate as to causes and policy pointers. The bad news is that no consensus has emerged. Those who believe that investment is fundamental to economic growth struggle against technologists over the role of capital versus ideas in East Asia's performance. Dirigistes battle free marketeers over the lessons regarding the role of the state in development. Jesus Felipe of the Asian Development Bank concluded his survey of the East Asian growth literature by arguing that "this work has become a war of figures. From the crudest calculations to the most detailed studies . . . [i]t seems that re-working the data one can show almost anything." We don't have a strong conclusion about the "right" policies that promoted growth in the region or, indeed, whether policies were central to the process at all.[5]

Just as confusingly, there is little agreement about the reasons behind the "failure" of Africa. In June 1996, *The Economist* magazine published a piece based on results from a global statistical study concluding that had African countries only followed better policies, the region would have grown 4.6 percent per annum faster than its historical growth rate—indeed, faster than many East Asian countries. A year later, *The Economist* published another piece based on results from a global statistical study that concluded: "For much of the world, bad climates, poor soils and physical isolation are likely to hinder growth whatever happens to policy." This study suggested that, even if Africa had followed better policies, it would have grown 2.3 percent slower per year than the countries of South and Southeast Asia. These two articles, with their markedly different conclusions, provide an illustration of the problems facing even the best development economists—in fact, both articles were written by the aforementioned Jeffrey Sachs. In East Asia and Africa alike, we know the plot, but in East Asia, no one can agree on the hero, and in Africa we're unclear on who's the villain.[6]

This is not to indict *The Economist* or even Jeff Sachs—or rather, it is not to indict only them. Thousands of papers and articles attempting to divine the causes of long-term economic growth around the world, testing hundreds of possible determinants, have produced results that are just as contradictory and inconclusive.

Nonetheless, recent analyses of country wealth have increasingly emphasized the role of long-term factors. Scholars now link present-day income with influences such as the mortality rate of colonial settlers in the eighteenth and nineteenth centuries, climate, natural resource abundance, and the extent of human losses to the slave trade. A growing mound of research papers and articles reinforces the conclusion that we know much more about the histories that rich countries or poor countries share than we do about the policies that will make poor countries rich.

In short, rich countries have a higher quality of life than poor countries. Poor countries are growing slower than rich countries. Many countries—especially in Africa—are hardly growing at all. And we don't appear to know terribly much about how to speed growth in those very same countries.

How, then, could one argue against the idea that development (whatever one's definition) has failed and Africa, in particular, is a region mired in a nightmare? How, then, could one argue for the central claim of this book?

One can do so by looking beyond income and pointing to evidence of widespread success in broader elements of development. Recent food-price rises notwithstanding, the evidence for any country being stuck in a technological dark age of population explosion and miserable subsistence without hope of exit is threadbare. Indeed, technologies of increased production have spread worldwide, and looking at almost any measure of quality of life *except* income suggests ubiquitous improvement. The general picture is of rapid, historically unprecedented progress in quality of life—progress that has been faster in the developing world than in the developed. This is true for measures covering health, education, civil and political rights, access to infrastructure, and even beer production. Since 1960, global average infant mortality (to examine something more serious than beer production) has more than halved, for example. In 2006, nine million children who would have died before then if mortality rates had remained at their 1960 level, celebrated their first birthday. And the vast majority of those children lived in developing countries.[7]

This broad progress might lie behind one other indicator that seems to be going up across much of the developing world—happiness. The proportion of populations in surveyed countries who say they are happy has been rising over time in economics that have seen rapid growth as well as in economies that haven't. Smile, and more of the world than ever before will smile with you.[8]

Evidence of widespread progress in quality of life applies also to Africa. This is not to downplay the region's challenges. Only in the last few years have we seen the horror of starvation and mass murder in Southern Sudan. Rwanda failed to prevent genocide, and Congo-Zaire, Sierra Leone, and Somalia long failed to create the conditions for normal life to continue. At times Ethiopia has failed to adequately feed large parts of its population. Zimbabwe has teetered on the brink of starvation, and cholera has reemerged in the country to kill thousands. These tragedies deserve global attention and a strong response.

At the same time, the proportion of the population of sub-Saharan Africa affected by famine between 1990 and 2005 averaged less than three-tenths of a percent. The proportion who were refugees in 2005 was five-tenths of a percent. The number who died in wars between 1965 and 2001 averaged one one-hundredth of a percent. These figures add up to stories of despair for many millions in Africa—but they remain stories of the small minority. For the rest, progress has been considerable. The percentage of sub-Saharan Africans who could read and write, just to offer one example, doubled between 1970 and 1999, from less than one-third to two-thirds of the adult population.[9]

There are other hints that income is not the end-all of development goals. The comparative experience of East Asia and the Middle East regarding life expectancy is a case in point. While we have seen over six thousand academic papers related to the subject of the East Asian Miracle, the "Middle East Miracle" is a topic in perhaps one academic article, where the phrase is used to describe a hoped-for future. Perhaps that's because the region turned in a particularly grim economic performance. Per capita economic growth rates averaged only about 0.5 percent between 1975 and 2000.[10]

But in fact the Middle East *has* experienced a miracle, just not one of income growth. Like most miracles—which typically deal with curing leprosy, healing the lame, raising the dead—this one involves health. When it comes to the miracle of life rather than the miracle of riches, the Middle East and North Africa lead the global pack, noticeably ahead of East Asia. Between 1962 and 2002, life expectancy in the Middle East and North Africa increased from around forty-eight years to sixty-nine.[11]

How can we reconcile the evidence of income stagnation in many of the world's poorest countries with evidence of dramatic advances in quality of life even for people stuck in those stagnant economies? And what accounts for the comparatively weak link between growth in GDP per capita and rates of improvement in quality of life? The short answer is that the biggest success of development has not been making people richer but, rather, has been making the things that really matter—things like health and education—cheaper and more widely available. It is the invention and spread of technology and ideas that have, literally, reduced the cost of living. A considerable majority of people worldwide have benefited more in terms of quality of life from technological change and the spread of ideas than they have from income growth. Even people today who remain as poor as their parents, grandparents, and ancestors back through time have seen quality-of-life improvements that would astound their grandparents and, in many cases, would have been beyond the reach of their ancestors, however rich they might have been.

For example, probably no country in the world saw much more than 90 percent of children survive their first year of life in 1900. It did not matter how rich the parents; the state of health technology placed a significant upper limit on an infant's chance of survival. The United States saw an infant mortality rate of nearly 15 percent, despite an average income that was one of the highest in the world at the time—a little above $4,000 measured in today's dollars. In this first decade of the twenty-first century, the country with the highest recorded infant mortality in the world is Sierra Leone, whose mortality rate is only 2 percent higher than the rate in the United States a century earlier—17 percent. Yet income per person in Sierra Leone has dipped as low as $404 in the recent past, or one-tenth the level of the United States a century ago. Countries as poor and wretched as Haiti, Burma, and the Congo have infant mortality rates today that are lower than those that any country in the world achieved in 1900.

Behind progress in the quality of life even in stagnant economies lie two factors: supply and demand. First, individuals can access innovations that allow for improved goods and services at low cost—more calories or better drugs for the dollar. Take growing access to vaccines. The percentage of the world's infants vaccinated against diphtheria, pertussis (whooping cough), and tetanus—with the DPT shot—climbed from one-fifth to nearly four-fifths between 1970 and 2006.[12]

The second factor behind improved outcomes is a growing demand for these technologies and related services. People around the world are better-informed consumers than they used to be. They demand soap to wash their hands, they want schools to educate their girls, they want governments that respect their rights. Consumers have learned both the value and the practicality of such service provision. We'll see that the demand for education is a particularly important part of the story behind climbing primary enrollments. Less than half of primary-age kids were enrolled in school in 1950, but by the end of the century the figure was closer to nine out of ten. Valuing ABCs and getting shots for DPT: These are the forces behind global improvements in quality of life.

But a final element of the story behind the spread of technology and ideas is the fact that governments are doing a better job at delivering services. Worldwide, countries are far more concerned about improving the quality of life of their citizens than they were a hundred years ago. The most corrupt and inefficient of countries in Africa are still providing services of a quality and extent far in advance of any country in the world prior to the Industrial Revolution. Even though teachers are educating perhaps only half of the kids in class, and more are absent, schools are getting built and staffed. Even though health care systems are laden with half-trained staff struggling to work with looted dispensaries, people are getting vaccinated and antibiotics are widely available.

On the supply side, advances in technology have made the provision of services more straightforward. On the demand side, the advance of knowledge has made such service delivery expected. A sense of crisis in development ignores these considerable successes in extending the reach of health services, education, and other basics of quality of life to rich and poor alike. That's the focus of this book.

These advances are no cause for complacency. Infant mortality may have fallen from 12.9 percent to 5.0 percent in Ghana between 1960 and today, but it is still at levels four times that achieved in Vietnam. The rate at which children finish primary school in Burkina Faso may have climbed from 19 percent to 47 percent between 1990 and 2010, but 53 percent of children don't have a full primary education. We can do better.

Nonetheless, the success of development in the past is all the more reason to believe that we can improve outcomes in the future. Africa is not an insoluble mess, a thousand-piece Jackson Pollock jigsaw with the edge pieces missing. It has chalked up some dramatic gains. And if it has done so before, it can do so again. Recognizing the success that the world has already experienced gives us some grounds for believing that future development programs won't go to waste.

And a leading role for technology and ideas is not to declare the irrelevance of income growth. No one should argue that countries where a considerable percentage of the population live on less than a dollar or two a day don't need economic growth. At the same time, an excess focus on income obscures the fact that for people living in the poorest countries today, the forces that have driven significant improvements in quality of life are technological change and the progress of ideas, not income. This is especially good news because, as we'll see in greater detail in later chapters, we don't really seem to know how to increase the speed of income growth. In contrast, we appear considerably better at improving the broader quality of life for everyone, at whatever income. A greater focus on proven approaches to more rapid improvement in health and education may have a significantly greater impact on the quality of life of poor people in poor countries than yet another quest for the grail of income growth.

Furthermore, in a final irony, some evidence suggests that a key factor behind long-term economic growth may be improving the quality of life of citizens—increasing their freedom to choose, their capacity to produce, and their expectations of living long enough to reap the rewards. Abandoning an excess focus on income as a catchall of development progress might, in the end, be the best way to achieve more rapid growth in the incomes of the poor.

The rest of this book lays out the case for relative optimism about global development. Acknowledging both the fact of a growing income gap across countries and the elusiveness of the quest for the causes of economic growth—the bad news—the following chapters still report a lot of good news. We have seen a global victory over concerns about perpetual poverty linked to overpopulation. We have seen rapid and ubiquitous progress in quality of life based on cheap technologies and the power of ideas. And we have a number of policy tools at the national and global levels to help ensure even further progress in the future. The beautiful banality of health, learning, and security has spread far, and can spread further.

TWO

THE BAD NEWS

Diverging Incomes

....

I n English villages around the year 1400, sanitation consisted
at best of a latrine trench or merely retreating "a bowshot
from the house." Many peasant houses had only one room, and
materials were flimsy enough that "house breaking" by burglars
was often undertaken literally—by breaking through the wall.
Wells provided the usual water source, and wood or dung the
main cooking fuels.[1]

In India in 1993, the poorest 40 percent of the population had
an average income of around $733. Out of this population, 96
percent used dung, wood, or coal as their primary cooking fuel.
Fewer than 5 percent had a pit latrine or toilet. They lived in
houses with an average of just two rooms, overwhelmingly constructed from traditional materials, and 80 percent got their
water from a pump or a well.[2]

When it comes to assets and infrastructure, poor Indians in
the 1990s lived in conditions not dissimilar to those of a medieval Briton. This similarity is not surprising, given that the
income of the average Briton is estimated at around $600 in

1500—a mere 18 percent lower than the income of India's bottom 40 percent 493 years later.

Poor Indians in 1993 had a significant advantage in terms of the goods and materials available to them. Twenty-six percent of poor Indians owned bicycles in 1993, although it is likely that horse ownership was lower than in medieval Britain. Ten percent of poor Indians owned a radio, 14 percent used electric lighting, and 16 percent owned a clock or a watch. This access to goods and materials unavailable to previous generations really matters to measures of the broader quality of life, as we will see. But the point regarding wealth remains: Poor Indians' income in 1993 was on a par with English peasants' income 600 years ago.

Since then, Britain saw average income increase more than twenty-fold between then and 1993, while India saw income only a little more than double, leaving many Indians today as poor as the average Briton many hundreds of years ago.

This is a story repeated around the developing world, a phenomenon that has continued to increase the gap between the global rich and the global poor over the course of the last century. It is also the measure used by those who lament the state of the developing world and point to the failure of development. This worldwide divergence in income—the bad news of global development—is the subject of the present chapter.

THE MANY PITFALLS OF MEASURING INCOME

Gross domestic product (GDP) is a measure of a country's collective earnings from wages, rent, interest, and profits. This makes GDP per capita a pretty good measure of average income per person in a country. But GDP is hard to measure, the numbers are very uncertain, and changing the rules regarding comparison of income across time and across countries can make a big difference in the resulting picture of growth and relative wealth. These problems complicate how we understand income per person in a given country.[3]

Once you start comparing income data over time, for example, you have to make a raft of assumptions regarding, say, the comparable value of a 1970s Ford Mustang and a 2008 Honda CRV to account for "real" changes in income. Over longer periods, comparison becomes ever more complex. Brad DeLong, an economist at the University of California at Berkeley, estimates that real incomes in the United States have risen eight-fold between 1895 and 1990. But in terms of the number of mirrors the average American could buy with their income, US citizens are sixty times richer today than in 1895. In terms of the number of silver teaspoons they can buy, the average American is actually poorer (by about 10 percent) than they were in 1895. How much richer you are than your forebears depends a lot on what you want to purchase.[4]

Historical data also involve estimates of GDP for periods before there was a national statistical office to collect the information needed to calculate it. Such historical estimates are based on uncertain data that require some particularly heroic assumptions to convert into incomes measured at year 2000 in US dollars. I can cite statistics that suggest average incomes were $1,706 in the UK in 1820—but just because the number is quoted to the nearest dollar doesn't mean it is anywhere near that accurate or informative about living standards.

The problems are similar if you try to compare GDP across countries. As anyone who has traveled between rich and poor countries will attest, money swapped at the local currency exchange goes much farther in poor countries than in rich. A *Lonely Planet* travel guide suggests you can get a large bowl of rice noodles in a Laotian restaurant for 60 US cents, and surely locals can do better than that. At my local takeout in Washington, DC, the cheapest noodles are about 7 US dollars. Using market exchange rates will give you a misleading picture of what an income per capita of $1,000 will buy you—143 bowls of noodles in Washington compared to 1,666 bowls in Laos.

The question, then, if we want to perform a proper comparison, is how to align the numbers so they come close to matching. The GDP and income figures used in this book are based on an idea known as "purchasing power parity" and adjusted for inflation. In other words, they are meant to account for the difference in the power of a dollar to purchase goods and services in different countries at different times. But such an adjustment, as necessary as it might be, adds an additional source of uncertainty. People in poor countries buy less stuff than people in rich countries, but also different stuff. And people in the past bought different things than do people today. This makes a big difference to estimates of relative wealth. If you ask "How rich is the average person in China if what he wants to buy is what the average American buys?" one answer is "One-third as rich as the average person in China if what he wants to buy is what the average Chinese person buys."[5]

Different assumptions about comparison across time and across countries, combined with underlying data inaccuracies, can add up to very different estimates of income and economic growth. Look at the recent immiseration of China in 2009. The reported size of the country's GDP dropped by a little more than a third overnight as statisticians recalibrated their purchasing power exchange rates—all the result of the compilation of new data on the price of goods in the country.[6]

In short, we know that present-day Britain is much richer than present-day India. And we know that present-day Britain is much richer than medieval Britain. But comparison of incomes across time and countries remains a complex and inexact exercise. We are not comparing like with like, and that can have particularly important implications for the relationship between income and broader quality of life over time, as we will see later in the book.

THE GROWTH OF GLOBAL INCOME

With these caveats regarding our measures of income, and despite the sense of development crisis based on such measures, there is in fact a lot of good news regarding global incomes. Average incomes per capita worldwide have risen from about $2,111 in 1950 to $7,614 in 2008—this, according to data from (the sadly departed) Angus Maddison of the University of Groeningen, the world's leading authority on historical trends in GDP.[7]

Furthermore, some level of income growth has been reasonably widespread. The United Nations Millennium Development Goal of halving the world population living on less than one dollar a day between 1990 and 2015 was met early, around 2007. In 1960, the proportion of the world living on a dollar a day was 44 percent, according to François Bourguignon and Christian Morrisson from the Paris School of Economics.[8] In 1990, the figure stood at around one-third of the world's population according to the United Nations. By 2007, the proportion stood at closer to 17 percent. This advance is due in considerable part to the rapid growth of two countries that used to be home to the great majority of the world's poorest people, India and China. Between 1990 and 2007, India's income per capita more than doubled and China's increased more than three-fold.[9]

INCOME DIVERGENCE

Still, averages hide considerable variation in income within economies. Alongside a growing number of billionaires, China and India still have around 670 million people between them who live on less than a dollar a day. And the rise of the Asian giants is perhaps less exciting news if you are a poor person living in one of the world's many smaller countries that have witnessed economic stagnation. The fight against global income poverty still has a long way to go.

This is especially true given that rich countries have, by and large and over the long term, grown more rapidly than poor countries. And some poor countries have hardly grown at all. Simply put, all countries started out poor—remember the income measures from Britain and India around 1500—but some are now rich and others are as poor as they ever were. In 1850, the richest country in the world—the Netherlands—had an income per capita of $2,371, about four and a half times higher than the lowest income estimated at the time (that of India). Since 1850, a number of countries have grown steadily—the Netherlands had a per capita income of $24,695 in 2008—while others have hardly grown at all. Take Congo-Zaire, for example, with a reported per capita GDP of $249 in 2008. The Netherlands' 2003 income is around a hundred times greater than that. And the Netherlands isn't even the richest country anymore.

Economic performance since the end of World War II echoes this long-term trend. In 1950, the poorest country for which we have data (Guinea Bissau, a small former Portuguese colony on the coast of West Africa) had an income of $289. The richest country in the world (the United States) had a GDP per capita of $9,561. By 2008, Congo-Zaire's $249 per capita ranked it as poorest. The richest was Hong Kong, with a per capita income of $31,704. The richest-poorest gap between countries grew from around thirty-three-fold in 1950 to around 127-fold today.

Because of massive divergence in income per capita over time across countries, the world is now an economically *very* unequal place. And this inequality lies at the heart of complaints about the failures of development. About 4.5 billion people out of the 5 billion for whom we have data lived on less than $10,000 a year in 1993. And the bottom 10 percent of the world's population shared only 0.6 percent of global income—an average of just $291 a year. Meanwhile, the richest 10 percent of the world's population controlled over one-half of the world's income, living on an average of $30,081 a year. Give or take, this is a 100-fold difference in incomes between the world's richest and the world's poorest.[10]

The picture is particularly stark for the continent of Africa. Many countries in Africa have incomes per capita lower than those in Britain at the time of the Roman occupation or in the midst of the Dark Ages. Africa's *average* current income is a little below that of Western Europe in 1850, and similar to that of the UK at the start of its Industrial Revolution. GDP per capita in sub-Saharan Africa rose from $477 to only $561 between 1960 and 1999. In the same period, high-income countries increased their incomes from an average of $13,000 to an average of $31,000. Sub-Saharan Africa's income measured as a percentage of the wealthy world's income fell from 4.8 percent to 1.9 percent between 1960 and 1999—a dramatic divergence.

The bright spots are tiny. Botswana and Mauritius have both posted impressive GDP per capita growth rates for extended periods but have a combined population of about 2.5 million people. More representative of the region's performance is the fact that the average rural Zambian will enjoy a lifetime income of about $10,000, compared to a lifetime income of around $4.5 million for the average resident of New York City.[11]

STICKY INCOMES

Given the fact of long-term income divergence, it is perhaps unsurprising that the evidence is strongly in favor of poor countries remaining relatively poor over time and rich countries remaining relatively rich. At the country level, Nepal is a good example. It was the poorest out of the fifty-three countries for which we have income data in 1820, and it is the third poorest out of those fifty-three countries today. Nine out of the top fifteen richest countries in 1820 are still in the top fifteen today. If you want to be rich now, it helps to have been rich before.[12]

What is surprising about this is that the income advantage of the rich over the poor in 1820 was so small in modern terms. The gap between the richest and poorest countries in 1820 was only $1,441. That compares to a gap of $28,030 in 2003. The former figure—$1,441—is less than half the income gap between Hong Kong and Norway—the world's first and third richest economies in turn—today. Adding $1,441 to average US incomes took just two years of growth between 1997 and 1999. One and a half thousand dollars just doesn't seem that large of a gap to make up. In other words, while everywhere was very poor by modern standards in 1820, very small differences in income in 1820 still have considerable power to explain very large differences in income more than 180 years later.

Wealth tends to stick to the same families as well. In the United States, for example, of those children born to parents in the bottom 10 percent of incomes, around one-third remain in that same position as adults and over half remain in the bottom 20 percent of the income distribution. Only one out of seventy-seven children born into the bottom 10 percent of incomes reaches the top 10 percent of incomes as adults.[13] If everyone worldwide had the same chance of becoming a billionaire, you'd expect the chance of a billionaire child having a billionaire parent to be one out of 9.3 million. In reality the odds are two out of five.

And before we spend too long thinking of one obvious exception, it is worth noting some things about Bill Gates's parents. While they were not members of the Forbes list themselves, both lived in the richest country in the world, he was a prominent lawyer, and she was on the board of directors of the First Interstate BancSystem. Bill Gates Junior almost certainly started out his life safely in the top 1 percent of global household incomes. Looking at it in those terms, we see that he didn't have too much further to climb—a point made by Bill Gates Senior himself. If Junior had started at the bottom, maybe he wouldn't have made it quite so far. Going from an income of a dollar a day to $150,000 a year is about the same distance as going from $150,000 a year to the type of income that might get you on the Forbes list of 400 richest Americans.[14] If Bill Gates's parents had been above-average citizens of Sierra Leone, perhaps his intelligence and determination would have left him a millionaire. An impressive feat, but not one that would garner quite the same global recognition. In short, if you want to be rich, be born to rich parents in a rich country. Failing that, at least try to *move* to a rich country.

POVERTY IS HISTORY?

There are exceptions to the general rule that poor people and poor countries today were poor yesterday, and fall farther behind the rich every year. We have seen that many countries in East

Asia managed what most countries in South Asia, Latin America, and Africa (sadly) failed to do. They converged on rich country incomes, reversing the trend of long-term divergence. Luckily, more recently, some of these converging countries have been very large. China and India have been growing rapidly, lifting many millions out of poverty.

If one believes that income is the primary force behind improvements in quality of life, one could see this as particularly good news. All that we need to do is to replicate the East Asian model in Latin America, South Asia, and Africa. The bad news, however, is that there is little agreement on what the East Asian model *is*, and even less hope that it can be easily replicated, with strong evidence of historical factors mattering considerably to long-term growth outcomes. That is the subject of the next chapter.

THREE

THE WORSE NEWS

It's Hard to Raise Growth Rates

....

I n 1949, the first World Bank mission to a Third World country headed to Colombia. On its return, it reported: "Only
through a generalized attack through the whole economy on education, health, housing, food and productivity can the vicious
circle of poverty . . . ill health and low productivity be decisively
broken. But once the break is made, the process of economic development can become self-generating. . . . [W]ith the knowledge
of the underlying facts and economic processes, good planning
in setting objectives and allocating resources, and determination
in carrying out a program for improvements and reforms, a
great deal can be done to improve the economic environment."[1]

In 1951, the United Nations produced a Primer for Development to illustrate tools and methods to plan for economic growth,
using an approach similar to the World Bank's recommendation.
An outraged Herbert Frankel, then a young don at Oxford University, complained in an issue of the *Quarterly Journal of Economics* the following year: "It is . . . precisely because the authors

of the report see economic development primarily as an intellectual or artistic exercise by leaders and governments that they
fail to do justice to their examination of existing realities in un-
derdeveloped countries. . . . [D]evelopment depends not on the
abstract national goals of, and the more or less enforced decisions
by, a cadre of planners, but on the piecemeal adaptation of individuals to goals which emerge but slowly and become clearer
only as those individuals work with the means at their disposal;
and as they themselves become aware, in the process of doing,
of what can and ought to be done."

Fifty-four years after the UN Primer for Development, Jeffrey
Sachs of Columbia University and the UN Millennium Project
reported back on a visit to Malawi. "Much of the one-sixth of
humanity in extreme poverty [is] trapped in a vicious cycle of
deprivation," he noted. But by "addressing a series of specific
challenges, all of which can be met with known, proven, reliable
and appropriate technologies and interventions," villages in
Malawi and worldwide "can be set on a path of development."
These challenges, which needed to be addressed in a planned
manner as part of a broad-based effort, involved (not least) education, health, agriculture, and infrastructure. Sachs's UN Millennium Project produced a report, *Investing in Development*,
based on such ideas.[2]

New York University economist Bill Easterly, a longtime intellectual opponent of Sachs in particular and of international aid
organizations in general, was outraged on reading Sachs's report
and demanded that we "discard the Planners' patronizing confidence that the Planners know how to solve other peoples' problems better than the people themselves do." He contrasted the
planning approach to that of a "searcher" who "admits he doesn't
know the answers in advance[,] . . . believes that poverty is a com-
plicated tangle of political, social, historical, institutional, and

technological factors," and "only hopes to find answers to individual problems by trial and error experimentation."[3]

Truly, there is no new thing under the sun when it comes to debate over development strategies.

This is not to say that there has been no progress—or at least no movement, progress being harder to judge—in theorizing regarding economic growth and its causes. The last fifty years have seen a blossoming industry in growth theories involving ever more formula-laden papers. If Greek letters per article are the measure of productivity in economic thought, output and efficiency in development economics have both grown immensely, because the topic involves a lot more calculus than it used to. But the question remains as to how much we have learned in terms of practical, implementable solutions to spur economic growth.

This chapter is about the failed search for the cure for economic stagnation, the silver bullet that would launch poor countries onto a path of sustained GDP per capita growth. It has been a grand search, involving thousands of economists across every peopled continent, lasting for at least a quarter-millennium. Many are convinced they have found the solution. But so, of course, are many astrologers about star configurations and technical analysts about stock price patterns—and they are wrong, too. Instead of uniting around one answer, economists recycle old theories into new solutions as the last consensus cure sinks under the growing weight of leaden growth performance. In fact, it appears that there is no single answer, nor a simple cure, with the past a considerable burden on future hopes of global income convergence.

THE HISTORY OF GROWTH THEORY

Perhaps the first recognizably modern theory of economic growth was the model developed independently by Sir Roy Harrod of

Christ Church, Oxford, in 1939 and seven years later by Harvard's Evsy Domar. This theory posited a straightforward relationship between investment and growth rates. Invest more in factories, roads, or housing, and your growth rate will go up. The more you invest, the more you grow. It involved a model—a set of mathematical equations—where you plugged in investment rates at one end and a growth forecast popped out the other. Many economists used the model to forecast GDP growth rates in the developing world. The World Bank's Revised Minimum Standard Model of growth (known as Rimsim to its friends), developed in 1972, was based on Harrod and Domar's work. The researchers based the model on the idea that each country had a "capital output ratio" that told you how much investment was required for each percentage point of growth. Countries with a capital output ratio of five, as it might be, needed 5 percent of GDP going to investment for each 1 percent rate of growth they wanted to achieve. Thus, if investment reached 15 percent in that country, GDP growth would climb to 3 percent. For a long time a country's capital output ratio was used by donors to calculate the foreign aid "requirement" of that country in order to reach a target rate of growth.[4]

But Domar himself argued that his model was not appropriate for determining long-term growth rates, supporting instead a model developed by Nobel Prize winner Robert Solow. Solow's model predicted that long-term growth rates were primarily dependent on technological change rather than on investment.

Economists define "technology" broadly—as anything that isn't capital that might affect per-worker growth rates. For example, it can include inventions as usually imagined, like the steam engine or the transistor, but also new processes, like the assembly line, or new ways of doing business, like double-entry bookkeeping. Solow suggested that as these technologies spread across countries, workers and capital could be used more effectively to produce goods and services. This, he argued, was the secret to growth. He also assumed that technology spread across countries at a constant rate. So, every year, the gap between advanced and backward countries in terms of technological prowess shrank by a similar amount. This suggested that growth was a natural state, if you will. All a poor country had to do to get richer was to sit there while the inevitable flow of technology from rich countries increased productivity and output. Later economists termed Solow's growth model "exogenous"—meaning that the dominant force behind growth came from outside countries in the form of the constant flow of technology. His model suggested that government policies or the social or geographical status of a country played a comparatively limited role in retarding or speeding technology flow—and so a limited role in fostering economic growth.

Solow still thought that investment mattered in the medium term. Especially in countries with many people, limited infrastructure, and few factories—a.k.a. poor countries—Solow's model suggested that investment would improve economic performance. Relatively poor countries saw higher returns to investment in the form of economic growth, Solow believed. As a result, poor countries would grow faster than rich ones until they were relatively rich as well—the model predicted at least a degree of global income convergence. After convergence had occurred, the world as a whole would grow at pretty much the same speed, determined by the rate of global technology advance.

Solow's model was exciting and elegant. Exciting because it provided a way forward, and elegant because of Solow's simple math. But despite the excitement and elegance, the model is not reflected in our more messy reality. As we've seen, the world has experienced *divergence* in incomes across countries. To deal with that problem, economists extended Solow's model. In this

version (Solow 2.0) analysts assume that the rate of technological progress is not exogenous to a country's economic system.
Instead, technology flow is an "endogenous variable," with a rate
that varies due to individual country features like policy or institutions or levels of education or health or trust in a society
(the variable depends on the economist's proclivities). This
adapted model allowed for poorer countries to grow more
slowly than rich ones indefinitely—at least until the factor or
factors restricting the diffusion of technology to a poor country
were removed.

In tandem with these developments in economic theory, the
1980s saw the evolution of a set of development policy recommendations that came to be known as the Washington Consensus. It was "Washington" because it was spearheaded by US
economists and policy wonks, and supported by the World Bank
and International Monetary Fund headquartered in the American capital. And a "Consensus" because nearly everyone in
Washington agreed about what the developing world should do
to kick-start economic development. Among the policies linked
with the consensus were devaluation, reduction of budget
deficits, liberalization of prices and interest rates, and privatization. What connected these policies was a belief that governments had played an overactive role in promoting development,
taking on tasks best left to the private sector and abusing powers
best left unused. According to the Washington Consensus, widespread government interventionism was not only unnecessary
to promote growth, it was the chief blockage to achieving that
growth.

Yet it was very difficult to push through Washington Consensus reforms, and when they were put into effect, they had limited
impact, encouraging the profession to look elsewhere for ulti-

mate explanations for low growth. If the reforms were right but not working, the problem had to be the reformers and the environment for reform. For an answer, many development economists latched on to Nobel prize–winning work by Douglass North around what he termed the New Institutional Economics. North's book *Institutions: Institutional Change and Economic Performance* suggested that a strong network of property rights, market systems, and decentralized, democratic decisionmaking structures underpin economically successful regimes. Some more recent offshoots of institutional economics have suggested a large role for economic and social networks that promote trust, highlighting the importance of such things as the equitable distribution of income and efforts to overcome ethnic divisions.[5]

Ideas came hard on the heels of one another. A simplified chronology of "what is needed for development" according to economic modelers through to the early 1990s might run as follows: physical capital (investment), human capital (health and education), policy reform, and then reform of government institutions.

The curious thing about these factors, new as they were to the formal modeling of economic development as it took place in the academy, is that they are *not* new to the less formal discussions of development that take place among practitioners and politicians. Despite the plethora of Nobel Prize–winning research on the subject over the last fifty years, the history of development thinking appears doomed to repetition.

Almost all the major potential causal factors that have at one time or another been plugged into models as a major determinant of growth are present as chapter titles in Arthur Lewis's *The Theory of Economic Growth*, first published in 1955: the right to reward, trade and specialization, economic freedom, institutional change, the growth of knowledge, the application of new ideas, savings, investment, population and output, the public sector and power, and politics.

Going back another century, we find that in some of the less emotionally gripping passages of *Anna Karenina* Leo Tolstoy writes about what was clearly an active debate in nineteenth-century Russia over the reasons for the backward state of the country. He covered topics such as education, insufficient market reforms to encourage entrepreneurship, and authoritarian versus participatory methods of development. Going back a bit further, to 1776, we see that still other contentions about growth are firmly rooted in the founding document of economics, Adam Smith's *Wealth of Nations*.

In other words, the Nobel Prize winners, the Washington Consensus, the Rimsim modelers: All were echoing centuries-old ideas. This calls into question not their sincerity or their smarts but, rather, their originality. Economists have (for good or ill) "formalized" their interpretations in their models over the past forty years. Now, a statement suggesting that a culture of thrift might encourage savings and (through investment) impact growth, as it might be, has to be expressed in a conga line of formulas before it is worthy of publication in the *American Economic Review*. The model—the mathematical framework—is new. But the insights, not so much.

All of this argues against the idea that we have discovered a missing silver bullet of development since the 1950s—or even the 1750s. At most it might be said that we have rearranged the bullets in the magazine. And while the elegant mathematical models do bear *some* relation to outcomes (no model would see North Korea following a pro-growth strategy), beyond conclusions obvious to any fourth-grader with a piggy bank, most theoretical treatments don't fit the evidence very well.

WHEN MODELS FACE THE REAL WORLD

In 1993, a powerhouse combination of economists—Bill Easterly, Lant Pritchett, and Larry Summers from the World Bank, and Michael Kremer at MIT—wrote an article suggesting why policy choices couldn't really account for patterns of economic growth across countries. Over the medium term, they pointed out that country growth rates are very volatile. Some countries grow fast in one decade and fast again in the second. Others stagnate across both decades. But as many grow fast and then slow, or slow and then fast.

What concerned Easterly, Pritchett, Summers, and Kremer was that policies rarely change radically over the medium term. Countries don't go from 10 percent primary enrollment to 90 percent college graduation rates over ten years. They don't even tend to go from very high trade barriers to free trade over a decade. So, countries that had high education rates in one decade tended to have high education rates in the next decade. Countries with high trade barriers in one decade tended to see comparatively restricted trade in the second decade as well. If policies change rather slowly over decades, but growth changes rather dramatically, that suggests policy change can't be the driving force behind changes in growth rates. The paper was titled "Good Policy or Good Luck?"—it came down heavily in favor of the latter.[6]

It appears that even dramatic "policy shocks" can have comparatively little long-term effect on growth. For example, recent growth research suggests that even civil war has little impact on long-term growth outcomes. Similarly, all of the bombing that the United States carried out on Japan in World War II didn't alter city growth in that country over the medium run. And two economists from Berkeley, Edward Miguel and Gerard Roland, argue that the extent of bombing of Vietnamese districts hasn't determined long-run performance in that country, either. In other words, even 7.5 million tons of explosives didn't alter long-term economic outcomes much at all.[7]

The Eastern European experience over the last eighty years also suggests that policy positions at the extreme of the political spectrum—from communism to free marketeering—may have a limited impact on long-term growth performance. Russian economic growth between 1913 and today has outpaced Mexico. And between 1950 and 1988, no Eastern European country grew as slowly as the UK, Mexico, Switzerland, Colombia, the United States, Australia, India, New Zealand, Peru, Chile, Argentina, or Venezuela. The economic (as opposed to social, political, and environmental) record of communist regimes wasn't so bad— hardly stellar, but better than many countries following distinctly more free market policies.[8]

The subsequent transition to capitalism did push a number of Eastern European economies to collapse. Russia, moving sporadically toward a more liberal economy, saw its average incomes almost halve after the end of the Cold War. Of course, models based on the Washington Consensus would suggest that Russia's growth rate should have increased as it moved toward more market-friendly policies and institutions. Meanwhile, China's gradualist approach to reform—the country remains officially communist— has ushered in the greatest decline in world poverty in history.

On the other hand, drawing any strong conclusion *against* rapid moves toward market models comes up against the problem that Poland, the Czech Republic, and Hungary all introduced stronger reforms than did Russia and have since fared much better in terms of economic performance. The universal policy prescriptions of dirigistes and interventionists suffer as much as those of neoliberals and free marketeers at the hands of the historical record.

Similarly with regard to East Asia, Australian economist Emma Aisbett suggests that the miracle countries should prove somewhat of an embarrassment to policy fundamentalists of both left and right: "Both sides claim the success of the Asian tigers as the result of their own policies, and the failure of many of the African states as the result of the opposite policies. Thus globalization's proponents claim China and Taiwan's growth in recent decades as the result of liberalization of their economies, while globalization's critics claim that these same countries have been able to capitalize on the opportunities afforded by globalization because of extensive government intervention both in the past and present."[9]

After the East Asian crisis, of course, and with remarkably little irony on either side, the statists argued that too much openness in the crisis countries was to blame, while the free marketeers decried excessive intervention as the cause.

As Aisbett notes, further support for an explanation that downplays the effects of government policies on long-term growth is the weak reaction of African countries to a range of different policy environments.[10] From state-led dirigisme in the 1960s to structural adjustment programs in the 1990s, average African economic performance was pretty grim. If the right kind of government was really the key to fast growth in Africa, one would expect that Ghana—interventionist in the 1960s and 1970s, liberal-reform-oriented in the 1980s and 1990s—would have seen significant growth in at least one of the two periods. In fact, Ghanian GDP per capita growth averaged 0.4 percent per annum in the first two decades and 0.1 percent in the second two.

THE ALCHEMY OF GROWTH ANALYSIS

Tests of modern development theories based on cross-country statistical analysis also suggest a fairly weak record. These tests examine whether, across a range of countries, and given other features of those countries, certain policies and characteristics are consistently associated with higher or lower growth rates. Production of such studies is a large industry. Google Scholar points to 14,600 papers referring to the analysis of cross-country growth experiences placed online between 2001 and 2007 alone.[11]

These 14,600 cross-country studies frequently use different time periods, different country samples, different statistical techniques, different data sources, and different sets of policies and country features in their analysis. If a considerable proportion of such studies nonetheless suggested that a particular factor (perhaps trade openness or education) was consistently related to growth, this would provide strong support for the universal applicability of a growth model based on that factor. Sadly, we do not see such a pattern regarding any particular policy or factor. Growth appears to be a more complex process than can be captured by universal models, and our knowledge of what reform will spur growth in a given country at a given time is thus limited at best.

Take the relationship between investment and growth. Countries often see low investment and high growth, or high investment and low growth. Looking at Zambia as an example, Bill Easterly estimates that if the early investment-to-growth models had operated as expected over the period from 1960 to 1994, the country should be very rich by now. Zambia had a reasonably high investment rate over those thirty-four years, and an application of the Harrod-Domar model discussed earlier suggests that the country should have had a GDP per capita income of perhaps $20,000 by 1994 as a result. In fact, Zambia's GDP per capita was $600 in that year.[12]

This might prove a worry for other theories given that investment has perhaps the closest relationship with growth of any indicator found in the literature. The comparative strength of the relationship was suggested by Ross Levine (then at the World Bank) and David Renelt in an early effort to test the power of various "correlates of growth." They pointed out that, out of all the measures they tested, only investment was reasonably consistently associated with income change over a thirty-year period. And yet it is clear that investment sometimes fosters more rapid growth and sometimes does not. Furthermore, in many cases, it might be the more rapid growth that is fostering higher investment, rather than the other way around.[13]

A weak association also applies to the link between education and growth, at least over the medium term. Lant Pritchett went looking for a link with economic performance using a range of different measures of the extent of education in a country and could find only a negative relationship when he could find one at all. He titled the resulting paper "Where Has All the Education Gone?"[14]

Evidence regarding global disparities in wage rates similarly suggest there must be more to being rich than being educated. A Nigerian who stayed in school until the age of fifteen and then looked for a job would earn eight times as much if she moved to the United States than if she stayed in Nigeria. That's why so many Nigerians try to move. People with equal talents, experience, learning, and drive can earn a lot more money in some countries than they can in others.[15]

WHY DON'T THE MODELS WORK?

A big problem with the growth theories being tested by cross-country analysis is that they assume all countries work alike—that policies that are good for growth in Uganda are good for the Ukraine and the United States as well. Francisco Rodríguez of Wesleyan University recently completed a paper that studied the importance of context to the causes of economic growth. When you look at the cross-country data, argues Rodríguez, it turns out that context almost certainly matters. But sadly there are not enough data to come up with robust findings that fully take account of context. All the GDP per capita statistics we have over the past fifty years are not sufficient to test the gargantuan models that result. The conclusion we can still make with some confidence, suggests Rodríguez, is that everything we thought was always related with growth across countries probably isn't always related with growth across countries.[16]

He doesn't give up all hope at this point. There is *one* paper that can be written using cross-country growth data that he thinks would have empirical merit, he argues. It is a paper noting that the answer to the question "What causes economic growth?" is not "investment" or "trade" or "education" or "technology" or any one "X" at all. Instead, the answer is "It depends." What causes economic growth in a country depends on where a country is, what it is like, and when we are looking at it. Circumstances are very important. Happily, Rodríguez has written that paper already. For every other researcher who runs cross-country growth analyses, perhaps it is time to shut down the statistics programs and play minesweeper on the computer instead.

Of course, along with most of the thinking about what causes growth, the idea that growth may be too complex to model isn't new, either. Forty-plus years ago, Nobel prize—winning Swedish economist Gunnar Myrdal argued that economic growth "concerns a complex of interlocking, circular, and cumulative changes." Myrdal in turn may have been remembering John Maynard Keynes, the dominant economist of the first half of the twentieth century, who argued that "we are faced at every turn with the problems of organic unity, of discreteness, of discontinuity— the whole is not equal to the sum of the parts, comparisons of quantity fail us, small changes produce large effects, and the assumptions of a uniform and homogeneous continuum are not satisfied."[17] And Keynes no doubt lifted the idea from somewhere in Adam Smith's collected works. Even knowing the history of economic thought may be inadequate defense against repeating it.

Once again, this is not to say we know nothing about the growth process. First, there are a number of factors that appear fairly robustly associated with growth—if likely as symptoms rather than causes. It is a near-universal phenomenon that, as countries become richer, the proportion of the population working on a farm declines and manufacturing and services contribute more to GDP. We know that expenditure on food as a percentage of total expenditure drops rapidly as people become wealthier.

Furthermore, we have learned that technology is central to per capita GDP growth—given that countries can invest in considerable physical capital (roads, factories, power plants) as well as human capital (school and university graduates) and still not see rising average incomes. We've also learned that some technologies may be more important than others in promoting output. In particular, given the divergence of global incomes, these technologies must be "sticky" in that they do not flow easily across borders as predicted by Robert Solow. This suggests there may be value in further analysis of such "sticky technologies."

INSTITUTIONS: STICKY TECHNOLOGIES

We have seen that "technology" as defined by economists is a very broad concept, covering all sorts of innovation. It covers traditional or invented technologies—Watt's steam train, Engelbart's computer mouse—to be sure. But it also covers anything else that can raise the productivity of labor or capital. Think of Adam Smith's pin factory, highlighted in the *Wealth of Nations*. The specialized machinery of the factory (technology "embodied" in physical capital) and the skills required to use it (human capital) were both vital, but what allowed for this specialization was the division of labor, according to Smith. "One man draws out the wire, another straights it, a third cuts it, a fourth points it, a fifth grinds it at the top." In such a system, Smith estimated that each small manufactory could make upward of forty-eight hundred pins per person, where one unskilled worker alone could make a single pin a day. The vital technology here is a "process" technology—the assembly line. Other such process technologies—a.k.a. institutions—might include double-entry bookkeeping, just-in-time management systems, transparent regulation, or even democracy.

Paul Romer, a father of "endogenous" theories that emphasize barriers to technology adoption as the reason for slow growth, suggests that it is process technologies that are the key to the story. He argues that systems like Walmart's management of inventory data have had a bigger impact on economic growth than inventions such as the transistor, for example. Or take the example of Toyota, until recently (when some drivers started to find its accelerator technology a little *too* sticky) the auto industry's most profitable firm. Toyota does not produce the most innovative or exciting cars (compare the Tercel to the Mustang). But it does have the Toyota Production System, which reorganized factory floors and pioneered just-in-time parts delivery, among other things.[18]

There is strong evidence to support Romer's contention that process technologies are more important to per capita income growth than "traditional" invented technologies. Not least, there is no relationship between a country's research and development expenditures in "traditional" or invented technologies, on the one hand, and growth rates, on the other. And the evidence from studies regarding the impact of war on long-term growth outcomes is a sign of the overwhelming relative importance to long-term development of things that can't be blown up. Process technologies can't be blown up, cars and computers can be.

More fundamentally, traditional invented technologies aren't sticky—they flow across borders. Transistors (followed by microchips) have spread to every country in the world—and very rapidly. Consider transistors in televisions and microchips in computers. Over one-half of households in the developing world own a television, and there are 219 million computers in low- and middle-income countries. Per dollar of GDP, developing countries have far more televisions and computers than rich countries. Similarly, you can be stuck in a traffic jam the world over, and some of the worst are in poor countries (Kabul, for example, has hideous traffic). Cars, televisions, and computers don't appear to be the kind of sticky technologies that must be behind income per capita performance.

On the other hand, there are no Walmarts in Malawi. And despite many attempts to copy Toyota's Production System model, most have ended in failure. Televisions and computers—along with cars, buses, and smelters—work pretty similarly worldwide. Inventory control systems and production management systems do not. They are highly context-specific. The same skills are needed to fix a television in New York or Nairobi; considerably different skills are required to be a good inventory manager. Furthermore, improvements in process technologies have to take account of the existing institutional context. Toyota's Production System approach is built around innovation as a constant but incremental process based on small improvements to the existing system, for example. This suggests a long-term and context-specific path of improvement in process technologies that would have the sticky characteristics we are looking for.

Institutions such as inventory management techniques, regulatory structures, or regime type might be central to the growth story. But the type of institutional innovation that spurs growth in a particular country at a particular time might be highly context-dependent. And given the interlocking nature of process technologies, it may be difficult to predict the impact of altering a particular process technology in a particular setting. This was, pretty much, the insight that won Douglass North his Nobel Prize in 1993.

HISTORY, INSTITUTIONS, AND THE DETERMINANTS OF MODERN WEALTH

In 1788 John Ledyard set off to explore the deserts west of Cairo, in Egypt. In 1791, Major General Daniel Houghton set out to cross the Sahara. In 1799, Friedrich Hornemann set his course south of Tripoli. None returned to report if they had reached the semilegendary city of Timbuctoo, somewhere south of the great desert. On their heels, Mungo Park, a Scottish doctor, tried to reach the city from the river Niger, which flows from the highlands of Guinea to the coast of West Africa. His first expedition, attempted in 1794, ended in failure—but at least he lived to tell the tale. After two years, a bout of malaria, and a months-long imprisonment, he turned back, exhausted.

Ten years later, Park traveled back to West Africa, accompanied by forty-one British troopers, an official artist, and his brother-in-law. On April 27, 1805, they set off from the Gambia, suffering under the unwelcome attention of powerful rainstorms, mosquitoes, wild dogs, crocodiles, dysentery, and, on one occasion, a pack of lions. By August 19, when they reached the Niger at Sego, five hundred miles inland, only twelve of the forty-three Europeans were still alive. And as they made their way down the river, more of the party fell to disease. Park's last known note records that his party was reduced to "three soldiers (one deranged in his mind), Lieutenant Martyn, and myself"—all of the rest had died.

Park reached the legendary city of Timbuctoo, but did not dare to disembark due to the threat from hostile Tuaregs. Sailing on, south toward the Gulf of Guinea, his last remaining boat was ambushed by Tuareg tribesman at the rapids of Boussa, three hundred miles short of the sea. Park and Lieutenant Martyn, the last two Europeans alive, threw themselves into the river and their bodies were never recovered. But it is worth noting that as many as forty-one of the forty-three Europeans died from illnesses—not from violence. And when Mungo Park's son Thomas traveled to Africa in 1827, to see if he could locate his father, he too was felled by malaria.[19]

Compare this grim toll to that of Lewis and Clark's troop during their intrepid adventure across the American continent. This began almost two years prior to Park's, and ended after his death. The party traversed the Rockies, navigated the Columbia River, and parlayed with Shoshone, Sioux, and Blackfeet. But despite equal exposure to local populations and a considerably longer time to fall victim to disease, the troop probably remained healthier than if they had stayed at home. Clark's journal reports the discomforts of the journey for his companions—at one point several men "had the disentary, and two-thirds of them with ulsers or boils, some with 8 or 10 of those tumers." Others of the party complained of rheumatism. But of the thirty-three members of the expedition, only one died—of a distinctly uncontagious case of appendicitis.

According to Daron Acemoglu and Simon Johnson from Harvard, alongside James Robinson from MIT, the altogether more pleasant experience of Lewis and Clark compared to Mungo Park has a lot to teach us about current levels of income around the world.

Acemoglu, Johnson, and Robinson have produced a theory of institutional development based on different experiences of colonization. They argue that parts of the world were extremely dangerous to the health of colonizers because of rampant disease. These colonies ended up with a very small elite of colonists sitting atop a mass of very poor people—either the original natives or imported slaves. This was the case in the Caribbean and most of Africa. Other areas were a good deal more pleasant for Westerners, often with (differently) disastrous results for the original inhabitants. There, colonizers and the diseases they imported would remove or wipe out the locals and occupy land en masse. Australia and the northern United States are examples. The resulting economies became considerably more equal. As one example, in the early 1900s about 75 percent of adult males in rural areas owned land in the United States, as compared to about 2.4 percent in Mexico.[20]

In a related vein, Stanley Engerman of Rochester and Kenneth Sokoloff of UCLA argue that the structure of colonies was determined by the products exported from them, in turn a product of climate and soil quality. Plantation colonies operated with slave and indentured labor; grain-producing areas were farmed by immigrant smallholders.[21]

It seems likely that both health factors and the nature of colonial production played a role in determining the resulting structure of colonial societies. Either way, when colonies were made up of elites of European descent on top of a mass of slave or indigenous populations, those elites had little or no economic or political incentive to expand infrastructure beyond that required to export crops or minerals, and a positive disincentive to expand educational opportunities, suffrage, or the institutions of economic development. As a result, such areas saw long-term development outcomes considerably less favorable than in colonies where the majority of the population comprised the descendents of the invading Europeans.

The same story in a more extreme form applies to Africa. Much of the continent was late to the imperial yoke, in large part because it was so unfavorable to colonization, as Mungo Park's experience suggests. Between 1695 and 1722, out of every ten soldiers sent to the continent by the British Royal African Company, six died in the first year and only one lasted long enough to return to Britain. Nonetheless, by the end of the nineteenth century, the great majority of sub-Saharan Africa was under the control of a small European elite exploiting native populations on plantations and in mines. Export commodities including coffee, cocoa, copper, and gold drove European investment in the continent and ensured that wealth was concentrated in the hands of the very few. Independence changed (somewhat) the nature of the beneficiaries, but did little to spread the wealth.

Nathan Nunn of the University of Toronto takes the argument over the causes of economic growth even further back, prior to colonization. He argues that Africa's poor growth performance is at least in part the result of the extent of the slave trade. Countries containing areas where slave exports were at their highest see some of the weakest modern-day economies.

Nunn quotes Affonso, king of Kongo, writing to Portugal in 1526 to complain that "there are many [slave] traders in all corners of the country. They bring ruin to the country. Every day people are enslaved and kidnapped, even nobles, even members of the king's own family." Eighteen million people were exported, leaving Africa with perhaps one-half the population it would have had in 1850 absent the slave trade. Nunn links the slave trade and related slaving raids with the collapse of existing governments and the persistence of multiple ethno-linguistic groups, and, through those channels, with weak institutions in the continent in postcolonial times.[22]

Bill Easterly and two colleagues push back the determinants of global economic progress further again—to technological factors that explain who were the colonizers and slave traders and who were the colonized and traded. In short, if your countrymen's forefathers weren't using a compass to direct their 1,500-deadweight-ton ships across oceans in the sixteenth century, your country is not rich today.[23]

Similarly emphasizing the role of colonial and precolonial history, Enrico Spolare and Romain Wacziarg argue that income differences between countries today are highly correlated with "genetic distance"—a measure associated with the amount of time elapsed since two populations' last common ancestors. The more recent the common ancestors, the closer the levels of GDP per capita. Spolare and Wacziarg interpret this as suggesting a strong impact of characteristics transmitted across generations (including culturally transmitted characteristics) on modern economic outcomes.[24]

Following a related line of reasoning, John D. Gartner, assistant professor of psychiatry at Johns Hopkins University, has written a book that suggests that Americans are rich because they descend from brave explorers and are thus "culturally and genetically predisposed to economic risk." To be fair, this book is based not on cross-country research but, rather, on brief studies of key American "hypomanics" from five different centuries. For the theory to have global application, we need to explain the development of other rich countries in the same way. The Swiss, for example, must just hide their hypomania and its causes very well.[25]

With nothing new under the sun in development economics, it is perhaps unsurprising that econometricians are now channeling nineteenth-century explanations for development outcomes. We are better off because we are better bred. Or, according to Robert Barro of Harvard, we are richer because we follow the right religion. Kipling would be overjoyed.[26]

On the other hand, the less eugenically or theologically inclined can look at the same data and divine an interpretation more akin to Jared Diamond's in *Guns, Germs and Steel* regarding the importance of *extremely* initial conditions. Diamond argues that the West triumphed over the Rest because Europe sat at the end of a continent broader than it was long, thus containing much larger contiguous ecological areas compared to the landmasses of Africa or the New World. As a result, plants, animals, and technology all spread much faster in ancient Eurasia than in Africa or the Americas. The *ultimate* answer to riches, according to Diamond, is not economic policy, politics, sociology, history, or even biology—it is plate tectonics.[27]

Among other geographically related factors, the absence of malaria, decent rainfall, and temperate climates have been put forward as important determinants of present-day incomes. In 1990, the average gross national product per capita of fifty-two countries that saw an average of under one centimeter of rain in their capital in any month was $2,475. For fifty-six countries that always saw monthly average rainfall in the capital above one centimeter, the average gross national product per capita was $7,320. Such factors perform considerably better in explaining variation in growth rates over thirty-year periods than do more traditional policy variables including investment and education.[28]

The development economics profession is excited by this new work linking climate and geography to growth via culture and institutions—but, again, we have been here before. Back in 1963 economic historian Robert Heilbroner was suggesting that such ideas were as dated as beat poetry and winklepickers: "Not many years ago the prima-facie 'evidence' made the climate theory of underdevelopment virtually the prevalent explanation of economic backwardness," he sniffed.[29] Indeed, as well as being among the most current explanations for development, climate-based ones are some of the most antique. In 1748 Montesquieu argued in his *Spirit of the Laws* that hot climates led to people who were too hot-tempered, cold climates to people who were icy, and the French climate to the perfection of Goldilocks in the realm of personality—and so in politics and life. In economics as in fashion, vintage is in.

A LONG-TERM ROLE FOR HEALTH AND EDUCATION?

Geography, history, and institutional factors predominate in explaining current levels of wealth, then. And the evidence appears to be against a strong role for education or health in explaining economic growth in the medium run. Nonetheless, there is still some reason to believe in a longer-tem role for health and education in determining levels of income. For example, Jeffrey Sachs and his colleagues have made a strong case that at least some of the impact of climate on economic performance may emerge directly through a health channel—not just indirectly through an impact on the quality of institutions, as suggested by Daron Acemoglu and his coauthors. In particular, the tropics are associated with more persistent malaria, and this has a significant impact on worker productivity. There is some further evidence discussed in Chapter 6 that links health outcomes to better economic performance.

And the importance of government institutions to long-term economic growth suggests a role for education beyond just that of creating human capital. Not least, education has a role in improving health outcomes, as we will see. And it can also teach a common language and instill a sense of national solidarity. At the time of the French Revolution there were over three hundred dialects spoken in the country, for example. An explicit goal of the highly centralized education system that emerged after the Revolution was to help foster a national identity. By 1919, it was a commonplace that "[p]ractically all modern nations are awake to the fact that education is the most potent means in the development of the essentials of nationality," according to an instructor in New York who had designed an entire syllabus for a course on Democracy and Nationalism in Education. Similar sentiments underpin the education policies of numerous countries to this day. It may be, then, that over the very long term, improved health and education may play a role in improving growth outcomes.[30]

Nonetheless, the short conclusion of this survey of the evidence surrounding economic growth is that expanding GDP per capita is a complex, context-dependent phenomenon reliant on intricate and varied institutional structures. As MIT's Daron Acemoglu puts it with regard to the growth performance of North versus South Korea: "We can be fairly confident that today South Korea is much richer than North Korea because of its divergent (and more growth-enhancing) institutional path. But we do not know whether this is mostly because of South Korea's economic institutions that protect property rights, because of its better educational institutions, because of its greater state capacity enabling the provision of basic public goods, because of its greater financial development, or because of the political institutions that South Korea developed gradually after separation."[31] Overall, we are far better at suggesting the fifteenth-century antecedents to modern wealth than we are at working out the policy keys to future growth over the medium term.

THE AFRICAN GROWTH EXPERIENCE IN CONTEXT

What does this interpretation of the causes of economic growth suggest about the performance of Africa in particular over the past 150 years, and about hope for the future? Clearly the bad news is that we know of no silver bullet that will launch the region onto an East Asian growth path. But it also suggests we may want to qualify our condemnation of African economic policymakers for their countries' poor performance. Well-trained economists without any political concerns aren't quite sure what to do either.

Historian Niall Ferguson claims that African governments have been worse for growth than were empires.[32] If we take the continent of Africa (and do not limit ourselves to the British Empire) the picture actually looks more positive than that. In 1870, prior to the imperialist scramble for colonies, the continent's average income per day was about $1.21. Toward the end of the colonial period in 1950, it had reached $2.33. In 1998, average income on the continent was $3.75. This suggests a postcolonial annual growth rate 0.2 percent higher than the colonial growth rate.

Of course, this is still a relatively dire performance, but comparing African growth rates to those achieved in other regions that are not hampered by a range of natural and structural barriers might give a misleading indication of success or failure. Growth rates have *always* been very low in the region. The worst we can say in fairness is that Africa has lived up to its historical record. This is a postwar performance about the same as that of the United States and Europe (where growth rates have been fairly stable over the long term), worse than that of East Asia (where growth rates dramatically improved from the prewar period), but better than that of Latin America (where growth rates fell).

And if there is a longer-term relationship between education, democracy, and growth, perhaps mediated through strengthened institutions, recent (dramatic) improvements in education rates and (less dramatic but still substantial) movements toward greater democracy might give some greater hope for the future. Again, if better health plays a role, as suggested by Jeffrey Sachs among others, this has also improved across the region. Already, as we will see in Chapter 4, Africa has largely escaped the Malthusian trap. Perhaps the slow development of stronger institutions will allow the region to convert an already strong performance in terms of absolute GDP growth into a stronger performance in terms of GDP *per capita*.

And even better news for Africa is the most important lesson suggested by the Soviet growth experience. This is that we shouldn't confuse economic growth with "development." Despite the Soviet Union's comparatively strong economic performance under communism, nobody would claim that Stalinist Russia was a haven for the good life. Beyond straightforward terror, massacre, and starvation, a range of other factors drove a significant wedge between economic growth and improved quality of life

in the country. Rampant pollution, for example, significantly affected health and lowered life expectancy. It is certainly possible
to see fast economic growth absent rapid improvement in the
quality of life, then. We will see in later chapters that the reverse
is also the case.

FOUR

THE GOOD NEWS

The End of the Malthusian Trap

....

Amartya Sen was born in East Bengal—present-day Bangladesh—in 1933. At the age of nine, he witnessed the Bengal famine, one of the worst famines of the twentieth century, in which 9 million people died. Thirty-nine years later, he published *Poverty and Famines: An Essay on Entitlement and Deprivation*, a book in which he suggested, surprisingly, that the problem faced by starving Bengalis in 1943 was not an absolute lack of food. Within the state itself there were adequate food supplies to keep everyone alive. Food production was only a little lower than it had been the year before, and higher in fact than during a number of years where there had been no famine. The reason for widespread starvation, argued Sen, was price increases driven by British military purchases, food hoarding, and price gouging linked to World War II. Landless laborers, the unemployed, and the worst-paid simply could not afford enough to eat as prices increased. It was not lack of food that killed millions but, rather, the subversion of the market mechanism. Sen's work, not least *Poverty and Famines*, won him a Nobel Prize in economics in 1998.

A dynamic similar to the one Sen discovered in Bengal seems to apply worldwide. The Irish potato famine occurred at a time when Ireland was actually exporting food—again, the problem was absolute poverty, not absolute lack of resources. Between 1979 and 1984, Ethiopia saw food production decline a modest 12 percent, while Zimbabwe saw food production decline by as much as 38 percent. Yet it was Ethiopia that saw massive famine while Zimbabwe, which had put in place extensive prevention programs under the recently elected Robert Mugabe, did not. The sad coda to this story is that in recent years, as Zimbabwe has slid further into anarchic despotism under the same President Mugabe, the two country's roles have been reversed. It is Zimbabwe that is seeing unnecessary starvation if, thankfully, not on the same scale as the earlier famine in Ethiopia.[1]

Sen's work and the analyses that followed have considerable relevance to discussions of the most effective responses to humanitarian catastrophe, but they also provide evidence regarding an even older debate, that over the so-called Malthusian trap.

Since the turn of the nineteenth century, the most popular vision of global dystopia has been fueled by the Reverend Robert Malthus's *An Essay on the Principle of Population*. A people incapable of stemming its urge to breed, Malthus argued, overwhelms a country's resources to the point that the only check on population growth is near-starvation. In the twentieth century, the vision was globalized in works including Paul Ehrlich's *The Population Bomb*, which warned, "The battle to feed all of humanity is over. In the 1970s and 1980s hundreds of millions of people will starve to death."

A number of people suggest that Africa in particular remains stuck in a Malthusian trap. Thinkers from both left and right use it to justify radical change in our approach to African development—an end to aid, its massive expansion, or even full-blown recolonization. Related to this, it is often suggested that the industrialized world's escape from Malthusian stagnation to modern economic growth contains important lessons for the developing world of today.

But if famines are the result of the distribution of income or power rather than of natural limits to the carrying capacity of the earth—as Sen's work demonstrated—this suggests we are still some way from the nightmare that kept Reverend Malthus—and subsequently Ehrlich and countless others—awake at night. Almost the whole world, including most if not all of Africa, has woken up from the Malthusian nightmare.

MALTHUS'S INSIGHT: THE MASSES ARE SEX-OBSESSED BREEDING MACHINES

The good Reverend Malthus was concerned with "the constant tendency in all animated life to increase beyond the nourishment prepared for it," which he felt "the race of man cannot by any efforts of reason escape from." Populations, he suggested, naturally expanded until such time that the limits to available resources dictated a mortality rate high enough to stop population growth. When checks to expansion were removed because of a "sudden enlargement in the means of subsistence," populations exploded, he argued. In the eighteenth-century New World, Malthus noted, populations had doubled in twenty-five years. If there were available resources, human populations no less than rabbit colonies would expand to exploit them.

The simplest version of the Malthusian model suggested that the birthrate in a country was set by customs regulating fertility, the death rate by income, and income by the size of the population. Lower incomes led to a higher death rate, declining populations led to higher incomes.

The relationship between population size and income was the result of the limits to land usable to farm. More people farming the same land would produce less food per worker. Any rise in population led to more people farming the same plot, with a declining return to their labors—and thus declining average incomes. As incomes fell, so rose the death rate, reversing population growth and returning populations to their equilibrium level. Malthus described how nature ensured that populations could not long outstrip this equilibrium level:

> The vices of mankind are active and able ministers of depopulation. They are the precursors in the great army of destruction; and often finish the dreadful work themselves. But should they fail in this war of extermination, sickly seasons, epidemics, pestilence, and plague, advance in terrific array, and sweep off their thousands and tens of thousands. Should success be still incomplete, gigantic inevitable famine stalks in the rear, and with one mighty blow levels the population with the food of the world.

In Malthus's view, populations inevitably increased until incomes fell to a subsistence level where birthrates equaled death rates. But "subsistence" did not necessarily imply income adequate only to provide the biologically necessary minimum of calories. Changes in the relationship between income and death rates as well as differences in customs regulating fertility could create markedly different subsistence incomes. If an innovation in health care resulted in fewer deaths at a given income level, for example, incomes of the poor would fall further as populations increased.

Indeed, Malthus argued that improved health outcomes by themselves would have little or even a negative impact on the quality of life of the mass of people—this even though he was formulating his arguments at the time that Jenner invented the smallpox inoculation. Malthus wrote, "As the actual progress of population is, with very few exceptions, determined by the relative difficulty of procuring the means of subsistence, and not by the relative natural powers of increase, it is found by experience that, except in extreme cases, the actual progress of population is little affected by unhealthiness or healthiness."

He was not, as a result, against inoculation, as he explained in the 1806 appendix to his *Essay*. Rather, he hoped that reduced mortality might encourage poor people to have fewer children. If customs regarding fertility were to change, then the country could move to a new equilibrium of lower births, lower (child) deaths, and higher incomes. "In making every exertion which I think likely to be effectual, to increase the comforts and diminish mortality among the poor, I act in the most exact conformity to my principles," he protested. But this was a hope rather than a certainty, because the birthrate would have to fall alongside mortality if any improvement to quality of life was to be sustained. "[I]n every point of view, a decrease in mortality at all ages is what we ought to aim at . . . if, at the same time, we can impress . . . children with the idea that, to possess the same advantages as their parents, they must defer marriage. . . . [I]f we cannot do this all our former efforts will be thrown away," because lower child mortality would only lead to lower incomes and reduced adult life expectancy.

In fact, the only hope Malthus saw for raising general standards of living was to change fertility behavior. If women started having children later, or increased the time between pregnancies, lower birthrates would reduce the population level; this in turn would increase income and so the age of death. In turn, Malthus saw education (which promotes "industry, morality and good conduct") as one key to the delay or greater spacing of child-bearing.

Overall, however, the Reverend argued that prudence in personal affairs, rather than institutional change, was the secret to progress: "[T]he truth is that though human institutions appear to be the obvious and obstrusive causes of much mischief to mankind, they are, in reality, light and superficial in comparison with those deeper-seated causes of evil which result from the laws of nature." Indeed, "the principle and most permanent cause of poverty has little or no relation to forms of government, or the unequal division of property." For Malthus, it was the rabbit-like breeding habits of the poor that created the problem.

HISTORICAL EVIDENCE FOR MALTHUSIAN TRAPS

If we dig into the historical record, we can find evidence in favor of the Malthusian model. In the UK, population size and wages shared a close relationship until around the 1800s. Wages in Britain (and across Western Europe) rose dramatically after the Black Death killed a large part of the workforce in the fourteenth century and then declined as populations recovered. Indeed, from 1200 to 1650 there was seemingly complete stagnation of the production technology of the British economy; GDP changed hardly at all, and any rise in population was offset by a proportionate fall in income per capita. More people working the same land made each individual worker less productive, as suggested by Malthus.[2]

From 1650 until the nineteenth century, innovation in the UK did allow for a slow expansion in output, but not at a fast enough rate to outpace population growth, so GDP per capita remained stagnant. Only with the Industrial Revolution did the link between population and wages break down, allowing for rising income per capita. The final escape from the Malthusian trap in the UK involved moving from a stagnant economy accompanied by cycling population growth to comparatively rapid output expansion (GDP growth) accompanied by declining birthrates, improved health, and a growing population.[3]

The exact nature of the relationship between rising incomes, declining fertility, and improved health in the nineteenth century in the UK is debated—all three changed at the same time, so it's difficult to see what caused what. Nonetheless, Michael Bar and Oksana Leukhina, economists at San Francisco State and Chapel Hill, respectively, suggest that growing incomes were not the cause of the demographic transition to low mortality and low birthrates. Instead, public and private health technologies (for example, sewers and toilets), knowledge, and ideas (hand washing and the Victorian cult of cleanliness) may have played a larger role in mortality decline. Meanwhile, declining birthrates were the result of more children surviving to adulthood. When parents saw their infants survive with increased regularity, they responded by reducing the number of children they decided to have in the first place. (These are issues that we will look at in greater detail in later chapters.)[4]

The foregoing does suggest a story that Malthus would understand—at least, in part. Improved child health combined with lower fertility may have played a role in increasing incomes. But Malthus missed the dominant role that innovation would play in both increasing output and reducing mortality, as well as the direct link between lower child mortality and lower fertility.

THE WORLDWIDE ESCAPE FROM LIMITS TO OUTPUT

For every other part of the world before 1700, long-term output growth remained below 1 percent, suggesting the stagnant

Malthusian economy at work. After 1700, North America and Australasia did see more rapid growth than that, but of the kind predicted by the Malthusian model (and recorded by Malthus himself). Two hundred years of economic collapse and population decline in those regions brought on by the guns and germs of the Old World were reversed as economies and migrant populations expanded to take advantage of the "sudden increase in the means of subsistence," as Malthus put it. Only with the advent of the nineteenth century do we see the spread of sustained GDP growth above 1 percent as the Industrial Revolution took hold.

The nineteenth century brought considerable diversity in GDP performance, with some regions including Asia and Africa seeing very sluggish growth while others (including Europe) took off with growth rates climbing above 3 percent. Conversely, the twentieth century has seen rapid GDP growth everywhere. And following World War II, developing countries saw particularly impressive GDP performance, with Asia leading the way.

In 1800, Malthus suggested that "[f]rom the accounts we have in China and Japan, it may be fairly doubted whether the best-directed efforts of human industry could double the produce of these countries even once in any number of years." In 1820, the GDP of the two countries combined was $249 billion. It took until 1952—or 132 years—for that combined GDP to double. But over the next 51 years, economic growth accelerated rapidly. By 2003, Japan and China's combined economies were thirty-six times as large as they were in 1820.[5] So much for land setting a limit to production.

More recently, between 1960 and 2000, among the 102 countries for which the World Bank has data, only the Democratic Republic of the Congo saw negative GDP growth rates. In fact, it was the only country to manage average annual GDP growth of below 0.5 percent. Only eleven countries saw annual output growth of below 2 percent between 1960 and 2000. This sluggish output performance in modern terms is more than four times the average rate for Western Europe as a whole in the Malthusian period.

The *laggard* output growth performers in the postwar period were Eastern Europe, Western Europe, and the Western offshoots of North America and Australasia. Africa's GDP growth rate between 1950 and 2000, at 3.5 percent, was higher than that of all three. Because it was accompanied by population growth (thanks in turn to declining mortality), Africa's output performance did not translate into rapidly increasing average incomes. Nonetheless, this impressive expansion hardly represents Malthusian stagnation.

The upshot of the story is that Malthus, at least for the period since the Industrial Revolution, was wrong. Not just wrong about Britain, but wrong about everywhere. Countries rich and poor alike are seeing output growth. Indeed, poorer countries are, if anything, growing a little faster. There is no evidence of the binding constraint on economic expansion that we would expect in a Malthusian world. There is no evidence that a limited amount of land (or a limited amount of anything else) has placed a ceiling on GDP. The whole world's economic output in 1820—at a point when Malthus thought we had reached close to the limits to growth—was somewhat smaller than South Korea's output in 2003.[6]

In the second half of the twentieth century, global GDP increased almost seven-fold, agricultural output approximately tripled, and population only a little more than doubled. Global cropland per capita has approximately halved since the 1950s, while daily food supplies per capita have increased by around a quarter. And worldwide, there are now as many people over-weight as malnourished (around 1 billion).[7] Combined with a $600 billion world trade in agricultural products, this expansion in both overall output in general and food availability in partic-ular has released even countries with the most limited farming potential from binding limits on the ability to feed populations. Malthus's "gigantic, inevitable famine" has been limited to cases where homicidal leaders prevent a response to blight or drought. In short, the whole world now looks like the UK did during the Industrial Revolution—technological advance has freed coun-tries from the curse of permanent, stagnant subsistence.

THE TRAP FALLS APART

Malthus's other propositions don't hold anymore, anywhere, either. He argued that there was an arithmetic relationship be-tween rising incomes and population increase. He also argued that rising populations would inevitably cause a proportionate fall in incomes. In real life, there doesn't even appear to be a strong *association* between the two anywhere on earth—including Africa, which is most often the target of Malthusian concern. Looking across African countries suggests that there is no sig-nificant positive link from GDP per capita growth to subsequent population growth. And countries where incomes rise fast don't see life expectancy increase much more rapidly than countries where income has increased more slowly (a topic we'll look at in greater detail in Chapter 6). At the same time, there is no sig-nificant contemporaneous negative link between population and GDP per capita growth—countries where more babies are born don't see declining incomes as a result. Once again, this provides scant evidence to support a theory that the region is caught in a Malthusian cycle.[8]

Nor is there any evidence to suggest that countries (rich or poor) that see improved child health see lower income per capita, as Malthus would have predicted. If anything, the evidence points the other way, toward a positive causal relationship between health and income. Improved health has also been behind the global decline in fertility rates. Average global fertility fell from 5.3 to 3.0 births per woman between 1960 and 2005, a decline that has now spread to every region, including Africa. Twenty-three countries in the region saw rising fertility between 1963 and 1967. Only one did in the years between 1998 and 2002, and the average fertility change across the region has been increasingly negative since 1973. It appears that what dominates the birthrate is no longer static custom but an increased expectation that children will survive and improved options regarding the decision to get pregnant. Once again, the driving force behind this change has been improved health innovations that have spread worldwide. And once again, this suggests that, the world over, demographic and economic trends no longer fit a Malthusian model of change. The population bomb is a dud.[9]

NEO-MALTHUSIANISM

While the classic Malthusian stories revolve around populations rising until the point that food supplies are inadequate, neo-Malthusian versions involve civilizations relying on unsustainable practices to promote growth. These practices lead, at some point, to environmental overload and social catastrophe. Consider the rise and decline of the Mayan civilization between 250 and 1000 A.D., discussed at great length by Jared Diamond in his book *Collapse: How Societies Choose to Fail or Succeed*. Between the mid–third century and around the eighth century A.D., Mayan civilization flourished—more people, grander monuments. In the city of Copan, now in Western Honduras, populations increased to 27,000 people at their 150-year peak between 750 and 900 A.D. Around this time, palace-building spread from kings to nobles, so that there were twenty palaces by 800 A.D., one alone of which had fifty buildings and room for 250 people. But the civilization was already starting to wane. Only fifty years later, social unrest had spread far enough that the royal palace was burned to the ground. One hundred years after that, the population of Copan was about half of its level at the city's peak.[10]

A number of theories have been put forward for this collapse, which may well have had multiple causes. Disease, invasion, social turmoil, and drought could all have played a considerable role. But unsustainable population expansion may have brought its own set of problems as well. In the case of Copan, to grow enough food, Mayan farmers cut down forests and cultivated land on the steep hills around the city, which rapidly eroded, blanketing the valley with less fertile soil runoff. Skeletal remains suggest the average health of an inhabitant of Copan began to fall as this occurred—there are more signs of disease and malnutrition in both nobility and commoners alike.

Greater agricultural and industrial output at the global level has created a growing range of neo-Malthusian concerns about the sustainability of present-day development worldwide. Such interpretations of future history make even Malthus's predictions look like a utopian fairy tale, involving all four Horsemen of the Apocalypse alongside floods, droughts, typhoons, twisters, and the potential for showers of frogs.

It is true that the modern global economy, 24 times its size a century ago and around 390 times as large as it was a millennium ago, is using natural resources at a phenomenal rate. Global copper output increased 23 times between 1900 and 2000. Output of aluminum increased 10,760-fold. Oil production increased about 380-fold.

Alongside growing use of nonrenewable resources has come increasing taxation of environmental systems. A number of major fisheries are in decline thanks to overexploitation. Annual world water use for agricultural, industrial, and household purposes increased from a little above five hundred cubic kilometers in 1900 to a level about ten times that today. World emissions of sulfur dioxide—the leading cause of acid rain—have increased from 20 million to 75 million tons a year over the course of the twentieth century. Atmospheric concentrations of carbon dioxide have increased from 295 parts per million in 1900 to 381 parts per million in 2005. Concentrations of methane, a particularly potent greenhouse gas, are increasing at the rate of 1 percent per year. Related to this, nineteen of the twenty warmest years ever recorded occurred after 1980. The increase in the rate of consumption of finite resources combined with the taxing of global commons surely raises concerns about the sustainability of the current trajectory of global development.[11]

Technological change and market forces may reduce the demand for, or reduce the disruption caused by, resource depletion. The operation of such processes in the past is what has given the lie to earlier predictions of imminent global environmental and economic collapse. For example, in 1980 economist Julian Simon challenged Paul Ehrlich to a bet. Ehrlich—author of *The Population Bomb* and an environmental millenarian—argued that increasing populations in a world of finite resources would lead inevitably to scarcity and so to price increases. Simon offered Ehrlich a long list of raw materials, any time range longer than a year, and a bet that those commodities would be cheaper in the future than they were in 1980. Ehrlich chose chromium, copper, nickel, tin, and tungsten, and a time frame of ten years. In 1990, all five had declined in price, and Ehrlich paid up, grumbling that he'd been goaded into a bet on an issue of limited environmental relevance.

But even if market forces play a role in adaptation, not least by eventually raising the prices of increasingly rare resources, the process of adaptation is uncertain. Global economic growth is increasing rates of depletion, and the transition costs (economic and social alike) of the switch to new technologies could be considerable. Take, for example, the recent rise in food prices that threaten tens if not hundreds of millions with poverty and reduced health. These are caused in part by US policies to reduce dependence on oil through increased ethanol production—an inefficient response to a genuine problem that has had terrible, if unintended, side effects.

The free market mechanisms that will control output of greenhouse gases, or threats to biodiversity, are particularly unclear. Even if there were an eventual transition based on laissez-faire, it will come too late to prevent a dramatic uptick in both global temperatures and species extinction. There is a considerable policy agenda to speed up the world's transition to global sustainability if quality of life is to continue getting better.

Nonetheless, returning to the concerns of "traditional" Malthusianism, it is worth emphasizing that the immediate concern is not a question of how many *people* the earth can support, but how much *consumption* of particular goods and services is sustainable. Even the current world population following existing consumption patterns is unlikely to be sustainable over the long term. A larger world population matching current US consumption patterns would be unsustainable over the shorter term. But it would be possible to sustain even a considerably larger number of people over the long term if they consumed in a more environmentally friendly manner.

How many are too many people for the Earth to sustain, assuming equitable and environmentally responsible consumption patterns? Historical assessments of the human carrying capacity of the Earth go back to 1679, when the Delft scholar Antoni van Leeuwenhoek suggested that the number was 13.4 billion people. Leeuwenhoek's estimate, unlike most things made in Delft, was not fragile—13.4 billion appears to remain at about the midpoint of more recent calculations. Reassuringly, this is considerably above current estimates of peak global population, which, according to the UN, will plateau around 2100 at approximately 10 billion.[12]

Production and consumption, rather than population, are the central concerns. Indeed, if we did want to limit populations on neo-Malthusian grounds, it is clear that we should not start by limiting the reproduction of the masses of the poor as suggested by the good Reverend Malthus. Instead, we should start with the largest consumers. Sterilize the world's billionaires first, then move on to a one-child policy for Switzerland, Luxembourg, and the United States.

For those subsisting on a dollar or less a day, more consumption is necessary to ensure a basic quality of life. And even neo-Malthusian concerns are beside the point when it comes to increasing the incomes of the world's absolute poor. Doubling the incomes of the world's poorest 650 million people would take the same resources as adding a little under 1 percent to the incomes of the world's richest 650 million. If we want a resource-neutral global income path we should get it not by locking the world's poorest into poverty but by taxing the rich.[13]

INNOVATION AND UNCERTAINTY

Rapid technological advance and diffusion are key to the global escape from the Malthusian trap. Technology has allowed massively increasing global agricultural production, and it has also allowed a growing percentage of economic output (even in the poorest countries) to come from manufacturing and services, providing other sources of wealth than farming. It has freed economies worldwide from the constraint of land as a limiting factor of production. The global expansion of economies rich and poor and the growing share of services and manufacturing in those economies are signs that the ideas and inventions required to increase output are spreading worldwide even while the institutions required to increase output per *person* have remained comparatively concentrated in rich countries.

Another set of technologies that have spread are a range of simple health practices that have played a considerable role in reducing mortality, as we will see, and this reduced mortality has been a spur to smaller family size worldwide. These advances regarding mortality have taken place in Africa as much as elsewhere—and so Africa, too, is on a path to significantly lower population growth.

Meanwhile, proponents of intervention still use the Malthusian trap as an argument to support "giant leaps" in aid-giving to Africa (the liberal stance) or recolonization of the region (the neoconservative stance). Neither approach can be justified—at least not by recourse to Malthus. Africa is mired in income poverty not by the laws of nature but (if there is any simple explanation) by its institutional history. This, and the fact that Africa in the postwar period looks completely unlike anywhere in the world before the Industrial Revolution in terms of economic and demographic trends, suggests that policy prescriptions based on Malthus's insights need retiring.

Again, fears spread by tomes such as Ehrlich's *The Population Bomb* and its many children have justified policy directions that would have appalled even Malthus. We have seen that he was in fact in favor of inoculations, for example, but in the late 1960s former World Bank president Robert McNamara discouraged financing of health care unless it was closely tied to population control. Otherwise, he believed, it would contribute to the population explosion. The decision to deny health care for those living today on the assumption that doing so would improve lives of others in the future suggests astounding faith in the moral and empirical basis of a deeply flawed economic model.[14]

This same lesson should apply to neo-Malthusian concerns regarding global sustainability. We should strenuously avoid the mistake that we sometimes made with population policies of sacrificing the health and well-being of poor people today on the basis of forecasts and estimates of potential impacts tomorrow. Our response to concerns of global sustainability should include the adoption of a Hippocratic approach: The threat should be confronted, but not at the cost of depriving poor people alive today of their access to basic human needs.

We may not know the secret to rapid income growth for poor countries in Africa or elsewhere, but we do know that the beliefs of a long-dead English parson hold little relevance. While populations have grown worldwide, the threats of both starvation and ill health have receded. The next chapter discusses evidence regarding improvements in the global quality of life in greater detail.

FIVE

THE BETTER NEWS

The Great Convergence in Quality of Life

....

Henry VIII, sexual carnivore and king of England for most of the first half of the sixteenth century, died at the age of fifty-five—possibly of syphilis, probably of an untreated case of type 2 diabetes. At about the same time in China, the Jiajing Emperor died of mercury poisoning at age fifty-nine, after a reign of forty-five years. Fast-forward to the start of the twentieth century. Queen Victoria died as the result of a cerebral hemorrhage in 1901 at age eighty-one—after the longest reign of any woman in history. Meanwhile, in China, the Tongzhi Emperor was born and died within Victoria's reign—he passed away aged eighteen, of smallpox. Vaccination against the disease had been made compulsory in the UK twenty-two years earlier. Moving to the start of the twenty-first century, we find Queen Elizabeth still hale and hearty at eighty-four. So is former Chinese premier Jiang Zemin, who is the same age.

The life spans of the regal and famous in Britain and China match the broader pattern of changes in global health over the last five hundred years. From short life expectancy worldwide in the preindustrial era, and deaths frequently caused by conditions we would avoid or cure today, health in the West increased and diverged from that of the rest of the world until after 1900—at which point, the rest began a rapid catch-up.

As late as the turn of the nineteenth century, Europeans' almost complete lack of useful knowledge in the field of public medicine meant that they could do little about reducing health risks in their burgeoning cities or in countries where they had yet to develop resistance to local diseases. This latter became particularly apparent in newly conquered empires. Remember, from Chapter 3, the grim experience of Mungo Park's expedition to Niger, where most of its members lost their lives.

The discovery and exploitation of a range of health technologies, combined with improved nutrition, eventually drove a wedge between European life expectancy and that in the European empires in the nineteenth century. But the worldwide spread of such technologies and of nutrition has seen the global gap in health outcomes shrinking again over the past fifty years. A similar story of growing global inequality followed by convergence in the recent past applies not just to health but also to education, rights, and infrastructure access. That growing equality in—and extent of—quality of life is the subject of this chapter.

THE TARGET(S) OF DEVELOPMENT

It may be good news that Reverend Malthus's dystopian vision appears universally superannuated. But this is hardly enough to declare the success of development. Even if Africa's situation is not Malthusian, it remains poverty-stricken. Around the world, about a billion people still live on less than a dollar a day and more than a third of the planet survives on less than two dollars a day. Whatever economic growth has occurred in the developing world has been insufficient to end income poverty, and, on these grounds, many states have failed their citizens.

At the same time, comparative performance in economic growth is surely a very narrow indicator of success and failure for a state. Income can buy a bigger house, a faster car, or a flatter TV. Wealth can ensure access to the powerful, the beautiful, and (cheapest of all?) the smart. Rich people can get higher-quality health care or schooling for their kids. And the taxes that rich people can afford to pay provide for roads, hospitals, police, and regulation. But what is valued about having money is the space, speed, and sleekness; the access; the health and education; and the convenience, safety, and security it can buy—not just a big number on a bank statement. Money is a measure of and input to quality of life, to be sure, but it is only one measure, and only one input. For example, by design, GDP only captures things that people are paid for—wages, rent, interest, profit. That means it misses things they aren't paid for—looking after their children, washing dishes, or growing food in their backyards. Also, GDP can only value government services at what they cost to provide. It is difficult to know how much people would pay to avoid living in a state of anarchy, but it might be more than the third of their income it costs many governments to provide.

That's probably why *Voices of the Poor*, a series of World Bank surveys capturing the voices of more than 40,000 poor people from around the world, suggests that the poor themselves see the escape from poverty as having many dimensions other than more money. Material elements—covering housing, land, and other assets—are universal concerns. But lack of access to education and infrastructure, alongside poor health, violence, and social exclusion, is also seen as a central part of poverty.[1]

In the same spirit, in 2000, the leaders of the world's states gathered at the United Nations to adopt the Millennium Development Goals, committing the international community to a number of targets for development progress by 2015. These targets included halving the number of people living on a dollar a day, as we have seen. But they also included ensuring universal primary-school education and reducing child mortality by two-thirds, reducing maternal mortality, improving gender equity, and increasing access to infrastructure. The Development Goals have highlighted the broader scope over which development success should be judged.

This broader set of concerns would be of little practical relevance if income per capita growth were a powerful proxy for improvements in health, education, access to infrastructure, security, gender equality, and so on—if increased income was the predominant force leading to better quality of life. And it is worth repeating that this is the common view of a raft of development economists. But in fact, the global picture regarding this broader set of concerns looks remarkably different from that regarding income growth—it is one not of divergence and widespread stagnation but, rather, of convergence and truly global progress.

The ambitiousness of particular Millennium Development Goals on health and education may mean that many countries will not meet the targets. In particular, Africa was "the only continent not on track to meet any of the goals of the Millennium Declaration by 2015," according to the United Nations World Summit Declaration of 2005. But it is worth emphasizing that within twenty-five years a country could have increased by 50 percent primary enrollments of the school-age population, or halved child mortality, and still have failed to meet the Development Goals targets. A country could fail to meet the goals and still have achieved progress over a quarter-century that is historically unprecedented.

In fact, this is the situation that a number of African countries find themselves in—considerable improvement even if not rapid enough to meet Development Goals targets. Halving child mortality may make the country a Millennium Development Goals failure, but still represents real success. That we have seen many such cases is evidence of continued, dramatic progress in quality of life that has occurred in countries both rich and poor, rapidly growing and economically stagnant. Countries and peoples are growing more similar in their quality of health, in their levels of education, in their respect of rights. And this convergence is not driven by stagnation of quality of life in leading countries. It is due to rapid—frequently historically unprecedented—progress in countries that previously lagged behind. This is how the world is getting better.[2]

CONVERGENCE IN GLOBAL HEALTH

Starting with health, over the last one hundred years the physical well-being of the world's population has improved far more than it did in all of the previous natural history of humankind. Global average life expectancy increased from around thirty-one years in 1900 to sixty-six by 2000. This improvement in health outcomes has been close to universal, affecting even the poorest of developing countries, so that there is strong evidence of a global convergence toward an average life span above the biblical standard of three score and ten.[3]

Across countries, the historical minimum life expectancy is around twenty-four years. This was close to the average for the

UK in 1363 in the midst of the Black Death, and was still close to the average for India as late as 1913. If that estimate is approximately correct, a strong divergence occurred between India and the UK as early as the fifteenth or sixteenth century. Divergence continued in the eighteenth and nineteenth centuries. The evidence for India and the UK, however, suggests that divergence slowed dramatically by the start of the twentieth century and turned to convergence sometime before the 1950s. India's average life expectancy was less than half the UK average at the start of the century and over four-fifths at its end—and this in a period when life expectancy in the UK increased by twenty-three years.

Christian Morrisson and Fabrice Murtin, who have studied global data on life expectancy and education stretching back to 1820, argue that the nineteenth and early twentieth centuries were a time of growing inequality in health outcomes worldwide. But since 1930, inequality has dropped dramatically below the level in 1820. *Average* global life expectancy has more than doubled over that time. All of this suggests that today's global population shares both the highest average level of health at any point in history and the most equitable distribution of good health at any point in at least the last few hundred years.[4]

Global statistics covering the second half of the twentieth century suggest particularly powerful convergence even as average world life expectancy increased from fifty-one to sixty-nine years. We can look at convergence of outcomes by studying the quality of life achieved by the bottom 20 percent of the world's countries compared to the top 20 percent of countries. In 1950, the 20 percent of countries with the lowest life expectancy averaged life spans only about half as long as those in the top 20 percent. By 1999, the poorest performers saw life expectancy two-thirds as long as that of the strongest performers—clear evidence of dramatic global improvements concentrated in the developing countries that were furthest behind.

One of the factors behind the convergence in overall life expectancy has been a similarly strong convergence in infant survival. Between 1870 and 1889, the average infant mortality reported in a recently compiled global database of statistics was 19.7 percent. Nearly one child in five died before their first birthday. If anything, actual average global infant mortality in the late nineteenth century was considerably higher than that. This early set of observations is among a sample almost exclusively made up of now-wealthy countries with very low current mortality rates.

Looking at a sample with far broader (and higher-quality) global coverage, we find that average infant mortality was 4.8 percent between 1990 and 2002. A conservative estimate of change would be that we have seen a 75 percent reduction in global infant mortality over the past 120 years. We have moved from one child in five to one child in twenty dying before their first birthday.

Once again, this progress has been global. As early as the mid-eighteenth century, northern European infant mortality rates were far lower than rates in countries such as India. To be sure, this was connected with tropical disease rates and population densities, but also with the fact that infant mortality rates began dropping in Europe at the very start of the Industrial Revolution. Still, in 1900, there were at most a half-dozen countries where we believe that infant mortality was below 10 percent, meaning that fewer than one in ten children died before their first birthday. According to available data, infant mortality in Europe as a whole averaged around 16 percent of live births. In Japan, Chile, and Mexico—and doubtless in many countries in the rest of the world for which we lack data—a quarter or more of children died before the age of one.[5]

Nonetheless, global convergence in infant survival, as with life expectancy, started before 1950, with evidence for India and the UK suggesting perhaps as early as the first decade of the 1900s.[6] By 2000, out of the 187 countries for which we have data, only 19 had an infant mortality rate of above 10 percent.[7] The worst performer in the world, Sierra Leone, saw an infant mortality rate about the same as the average for Europe a hundred years earlier. In 2000, 46 countries had infant mortality rates below 1 percent, one-tenth the level of the global leaders in 1900. Some countries have achieved truly spectacular gains. In Chile, mortality dropped from 25 percent to 1 percent of infants over the course of the twentieth century. In Japan, it fell from 25 percent to 0.3 percent over those same hundred years. But the recent past in particular has seen widespread progress in every region of the world. Eighty percent of countries for which we have data have seen infant mortality more than halve between 1960 and 2005.[8]

The global convergence in a number of health outcomes including life expectancy has slowed in the recent past. China, despite rapidly growing wealth, saw stagnating rural health outcomes in the 1990s. And it is hard to exaggerate the tragic impact that AIDS has had, and will continue to have, on life expectancy in the sub-Saharan region as a whole. Life expectancy in the region has almost stagnated since 1985.

Nonetheless, in absolute terms, and despite almost no economic growth and the impact of the AIDS epidemic, African countries have seen a greater absolute increase in life expectancy than high-income countries since 1960—a 13-year increase. Similarly, Africa has shared in progress on infant and child health.

The survival rate of children under five years old since 1965 increased from seventy-five to eighty-eight out of every one hundred children born in sub-Saharan Africa. In percentage and absolute terms, sub-Saharan Africa's improvement was far more impressive than that in high-income countries, suggesting rapid convergence. The region has achieved these successes while its population has increased more than three-fold. Africa has many more people who are enjoying a better quality of health.[9]

This translates into millions fewer stories of tragedy and distress for the region's families. Take the case of just one country—landlocked Niger, 80 percent desert and one of the poorest countries in the world, where Mungo Park's expedition suffered much of its terrible death toll. This is a country that has seen its income shrinking over the past few decades. But around eight hundred children were born last week in Niger who will survive to their first birthday due to improvements in child health outcomes since 1960.

CONVERGENCE IN EDUCATION

A similar story can be told regarding the ability to read and write. Illiteracy is rapidly becoming a curable condition of youth rather than a chronic condition of adulthood worldwide.

By the time of the first daily newspaper, printed in London starting in 1702, it is very likely that the great divergence in global literacy levels had begun. By 1850, UK literacy levels were already around three-quarters of the adult population, a rate that was similar to US rates and slightly lower than levels in Prussia. In Argentina and Chile, literacy was limited to between one-fifth and one-quarter of the population. And rates in most of the rest of the developing world (including India) were well below one in ten.

But convergence also began very early, almost certainly in the nineteenth century. In Argentina, literacy had increased to 73 percent of the population by 1925, and in Chile it reached 66 percent that same year. By 1913, adult literacy in India was at 9 percent, and certainly at least since then, the picture has been one of rapid convergence with the UK.[10]

In the eighty years between 1870 and 1950, the proportion of the world's population able to read increased from one-quarter to one-half, and from 1950 to 2000, it increased to four-fifths of the global population. Between 1950 and 1999, the bottom 20 percent of countries increased their literacy rates as a proportion of rates in the top 20 percent, from one-eighth to more than one-half.[11]

Progress has been particularly heartening for women. Between 1970 and 2000, the global average ratio of female to male literacy has improved from 59 to 80 percent. And Africa has again been fast catching up with the near-universal adult literacy of high-income countries. Literacy rates in the sub-Saharan region increased from 28 to 61 percent between 1970 and the close of the century.

One major factor behind global increases in literacy has been far more widespread access to education. The idea of universal education stretches back at least as far as the European Reformation, with the Protestant focus on reading the Bible an important spur. In Scotland in 1561, John Knox called for the "virtuous education and godly upbringing of the youth of this Realm," involving a schoolmaster to be appointed to every church. "For the poor," he argued "if need be, education may be given free; for the rich, it is only necessary to see that education is given under proper supervision."

Motivated by similar principles, Connecticut and the Massachusetts Bay Colony in North America were the first places in the world to mandate universal elementary schooling in the 1640s and '50s. De jure requirements for universal education spread over the next two hundred and fifty years. German imperial edicts called for community-funded universal education in the 1760s, and one of the early acts of the French Revolutionary government was to call for universal state education for boys to the age of eighteen (although no funds were provided for the purpose).

Unsurprisingly, de facto enrollment rates usually trailed behind the de jure requirements. Nonetheless, by 1870, primary enrollment was around 50 percent in the UK, 67 percent in Germany, and 75 percent in the United States. Enrollment rates elsewhere in the world remained low. Somewhere between 12 and 23 percent of the world's children aged five to fourteen were enrolled in a school, but the rate was only 6 percent in Brazil and 2 percent in India.

By 1930, primary enrollment had reached 11 percent in India and 22 percent in Brazil. African countries in particular still remained far behind. With few exceptions, colonial administrations made little effort to expand access to education beyond that provided by a scattering of mission schools. A few countries—including Ghana, Kenya, Malawi, South Africa, and Zimbabwe—saw primary enrollment levels climb above 5 percent prior to World War II. The rest did not.

The postwar period saw an explosion in access levels even in Africa, a trend continued in the postindependence period. Côte d'Ivoire saw enrollments climb from about 5 to 40 percent in the 1950s, for example. More widely, by 1950, global average enrollment levels had increased to 47 percent, reflecting close to universal levels in Western Europe, but also rapid strides in enrollment in much of the rest of the world. By 2002, global net primary enrollment was around 87 percent, with a little under

one-half of the world's countries having achieved universal enrollment levels.[12]

Other indicators of educational progress also show strong evidence of growth and convergence over the last one hundred
years. The average number of years an adult has spent in school
(from primary through university) is often chosen as the best
measure of a country's "human capital stock" (yes, this is how social scientists talk about education and knowledge). And this average schooling statistic across countries increased from around
two years in 1900 to above seven years by the end of the century.[13]

In 1900, the bottom fifth of countries—the laggards in terms
of human capital—saw education rates that suggested the average adult had been in school for less than two months. Of
course, this reflected the fact that the great majority of adults
had never set foot in a classroom at all, that education was the
privilege of a small elite. In contrast, the top fifth of countries in
1900 already had average human capital stocks of over seven
years, suggesting that the considerable majority of citizens had
completed primary schooling, at the least. The gap between leaders and laggards in 1900 was huge: a forty-fold difference in average educational levels.

Since then, leader countries have extended access to secondary and tertiary education, and the average number of years that
citizens of those countries spend in school has nearly doubled
to thirteen years. But education rates in laggard countries have
exploded. Average human capital levels in the least-educated
fifth of countries increased nineteen times over the course of
the century as basic education evolved from a luxury to ubiquity.
Progress was particularly rapid in the period between the end
of World War II to the end of the 1970s, but even the "lost development decades" of the 1980s and 1990s saw average years
of education in these laggard countries increase from around

one year and four months to two years and eight months. Laggard countries are still behind, of course, but they went from having around one-fortieth of the human capital stocks of leader countries in 1900 to about one-quarter by the year 2000.

Progress may be even more rapid than presented what is in international educational statistics. Not least, official statistics can dramatically undercount the number of children in private schooling in developing countries. In Lagos State in Nigeria, for example, as many as 75 percent of schoolchildren are in private schools, with a larger proportion of all students in unregistered private schools (33 percent of the total) than in government schools (25 percent). The official statistics do not include these unregistered schools, despite the fact that many of them may be providing a better quality of education than government schools.[14]

POLITICAL AND CIVIL RIGHTS

A possible factor behind improvements in social indicators is the advance of civil and political rights, at least as far as available data suggest.

For most people for the great majority of history, basic liberties have been at least curtailed—often to the point that it is easier to highlight where freedoms were granted than where they were denied. Think of the democratic city-state of Athens (assuming you were male, you were Athenian, and you believed in the Ancestral Gods), or the Moorish Kingdom of Spain, where the caliphs provided for religious freedom (although they weren't so keen on democracy).

But the last two hundred years have seen a considerable expansion in both the idea and practice of liberty. For example, we have moved from a world where as much as 38 percent of the population was enslaved in the US South alone in 1750 to one

where slavery is outlawed everywhere. Much of this progress occurred over the course of the nineteenth century, although slavery only finally legally died out in the past three decades with
abolition in countries including Yemen, Mauritania, Saudi Arabia, and Qatar.

Progress in enshrining rights particularly as a legal principle
has been dramatic since World War II. En masse, countries have
signed on to 1948 UN Universal Declaration of Human Rights,
the 1950 European Convention for the Protection of Human
Rights, the 1953 Convention on the Political Rights of Women,
the 1966 UN International Covenant on Civil and Political
Rights, the 1967 Convention on the Elimination of Discrimination Against Women, the 1986 African Charter on Human and
Peoples' Rights, and so on. The overwhelming majority of people
worldwide now live in countries that have signed on to the Declaration of Human Rights. (A comparatively recent event extending global population coverage was the accession of the People's
Republic of China in 1971.)

Furthermore, the great majority of the world's constitutions
include lengthy sections regarding the rights of individuals. Take,
for example, Zimbabwe's constitution, which guarantees liberty,
freedom of conscience, speech, movement, and assembly, and
due and rapid process under law, all while it bans discriminatory
laws, undue search, slavery, and forced labor alongside torture
and degrading punishment. Of course, the example of Zimbabwe
also illustrates how limited the impact of such language can be
on behavior. The country's recent history has seen significant
violations of the majority of these rights. Nonetheless, the spread
of constitutional guarantees regarding rights suggests that they
are far more often abused either extrajudicially or with the con-
nivance of the judiciary rather than that rights frameworks are
merely absent from national legal institutions.[15]

On the side of political rights, universal suffrage and political sovereignty are, in practice, twentieth-century inventions and have spread haltingly in the last one hundred years. To take but two examples, Brazil finally abandoned a literacy qualification for suffrage in 1988, and Switzerland allowed women to vote only in 1971. Lebanon retains a literacy requirement on women voters to this day, and Saudi Arabia still doesn't allow women to vote at all. Of course, Saudi democracy spreads only as far as local elections, and this illustrates another area of halting progress—toward having something important to vote *for*. As with civil rights, the idea of popular sovereignty is an old one, but its application remains patchy to this day. North Korea has both universal suffrage and very high (legally required) turnout. Still, any actual impact of this widespread voting on the direction of the country is perhaps hard to detect.

Nonetheless, the end of slavery, the adoption of human rights covenants, and the spread of electoral systems do provide evidence for some global progress in civil and political rights over the last two centuries. And the fact that the rights are enshrined in constitutions does help frame expectations—and so the demand that rights are respected. This is reflected in a growing number of countries actually practicing what they have signed on to in terms of rights, a picture that we can confirm by studying data on the extent of such rights over that two-hundred-year period.

Putting a numerical value to civil and political rights is a subjective science, but one of the more widely accepted measures is provided by the Polity database maintained by political scientists at George Mason University. The Polity measure reflects the level of democracy or autocracy in a country on a scale from −10 to +10 (from strong autocracy to strong democracy). A fully democratic government under the Polity measure has three essential

elements: fully competitive political participation, institution-
alized constraints on executive power, and a guarantee of civil
liberties to all citizens in their daily lives and in political participation. The Polity indicator is an imperfect measure of democracy, taking no account of rates of enfranchisement, for example.
(Countries that deny votes to women can score a perfect 10.)
Furthermore, it does not cover colonies. Despite this, its geographic and historic coverage is very wide, and it has at least
some credibility among political scientists as a gauge of rights
observance.

The proportion of the world's population covered by Polity
has reached close to 100 percent (160 countries), up from 51
percent (35 countries) in 1820. A considerable part of that early
uncovered population lived in colonial systems or areas not recognizably part of a state system. In these environments, participation in political systems was (usually) extremely limited. Yet
the average global Polity score has increased from −6.7 in 1820
to +2.9 in 2000. If we assume that areas not included in the database would score −10, an adjusted Polity score suggests even
more dramatic improvement in global civil and political rights,
of more than 11 points on the 20-point scale. Also worth noting
is the cycle away from the lowest score to the highest. In 1820,
37 percent of countries scored −10. By 2000, this was only 1 percent. In 1820, no country scored 10; by 2000, 21 percent of countries had a perfect score.

The Polity data for the postwar period provide strong evidence of both convergence and continued improvement. In 1950
the average Polity score for the seventy-one countries with data
was 0.3. As a number of regimes fell into autocracy in the 1960s
and '70s, the average score for this group of seventy-one countries fell, but by 2002 the score had recovered and surpassed earlier performance, reaching 5.5. The average global Polity score

across countries has never been as high as it is today, nor has the percentage of countries scoring a perfect 10. There are large parts of the world where rights remain severely and often violently curtailed (not least China), but the global trend is away from autocracy and toward respect for civil and political rights. And once again there was faster improvement in previously more autocratic regimes.[16]

VIOLENCE

Over the very long term, the world is a considerably more peaceful place than it was before the agricultural revolution, when somewhere between 5 and 30 percent of deaths were probably caused by violence. And the world as a whole today is also comparatively crime-free compared to Britain in the Middle Ages, when homicide rates were around 23 per 100,000. The global average is one-third that level today.[17]

Still, evidence from a global sample of countries suggests that the homicide rate increased from 5 to 7 per 100,000 people per year between the late 1970s and the early 1990s. Violent crime increased particularly dramatically in countries in Latin America and the Caribbean that are connected to the international drug trade. Violent crime in Jamaica increased 150 percent between 1977 and 2000, for example. And the proportion of people dying in wars each year also grew from as few as 1 percent of deaths in the nineteenth century to perhaps as many as 4 percent in the twentieth. Governments killed as many as 170 million civilians from 1900 to 1987.[18]

The good news is that the tide appears to have turned since the end of the Cold War, with regard to violence both within and across countries. The number of battle deaths in interstate wars has declined from more than 65,000 per year in the 1950s to fewer than 2,000 per year in the current decade. Iraq's invasion of Kuwait was perhaps the only explicit war of conquest in the postwar period. And "traditional" wars that pit two states against each other in a battle over land and resources are also almost completely extinct—a recent sputtering exception being the conflict between Ethiopia and Eritrea. Most remaining international wars of the last ten years have involved "police actions," many approved by the UN Security Council.[19]

Measures that include civil war suggest that the period around 1900 was still more peaceful than today, and horrific conflicts are ongoing not least in the Congo. But the number of major civil and international wars being fought also declined from twenty-six to four between 1991 and 2005.[20]

CONVERGENCE IN OTHER INDICATORS

Turning to a number of other socioeconomic indicators, we find that the picture remains broadly positive regarding both progress and convergence. Regarding income equality within countries, not least, unequal societies have seen some relative improvement in income distribution compared to countries that began the period more equal, according to the available global data— that is, the gap between rich and poor within a given country is growing narrower.

We have also seen that one measure of gender equality, female literacy as a percentage of male literacy, suggests rapid global convergence, in this case alongside rapid global improvement. Another measure of gender equity, the percentage of seats held by women in national parliaments, increased from 13 to 19 percent worldwide between 1990 and 2010, with (once again) more rapid progress in those countries where women were previously particularly underrepresented.

Of course, with women representing about half of the global population, there is room for considerable improvement, and violations of women's rights remain some of the most common and pernicious worldwide. By far the most ubiquitous violence occurs within the household. A range of surveys suggests that across countries between 10 and 50 percent of women have been beaten or physically mistreated by a current or former partner. But broad progress in measures of gender equality at least implies some hope that these abuses may decline in the future.[21]

Inflation, usually included in "misery indices" of economic discontent, actually increased according to a weighted average global measure between 1965 and 1999 (although it is down from its peak in the late 1970s and early 1980s). Despite that, evidence again suggests convergence, with hyperinflation now limited to a few standout countries such as Zimbabwe in recent years. Turning to an indicator that may have a place in an index of economic contentment, and certainly gives hints as to growing levels of "non-necessary" consumption, we find that beer production per capita worldwide has nearly doubled on a weighted average basis from 1950 to 1990, while global variation in production has fallen. The bottom 20 percent of the world has almost quintupled its beer production over those forty years compared to the top 20 percent of the world.

LIFE IS FAR FROM PERFECT—BUT IT IS BETTER

A colleague who was once on a World Health Organization expert committee discussing mortality data suggested something about the quality of at least some of the mortality statistics we use: "[A]fter a couple of days of discussion, one of our members took the floor and said he didn't understand why we were spending so much time on the subject. He said he was responsible for reporting on child survival for his country, and each year he simply looked at the estimate of the previous year and adjusted it in the direction he thought reasonable." And thus we should be wary of taking any mortality statistics as fully and accurately representing the state of the world.[22]

But we should not overplay the data problem. For many quality-of-life indicators, the changes over time have been so dramatic that we can be confident that apparent change is not driven simply by measurement error. Even accounting for data concerns, robust patterns of change emerge across a range of indicators covering health, education, gender equality, war deaths, and political and civil rights.

There are caveats to the broadly positive picture of improvement and convergence. First off, rates of both global growth and global convergence in quality of life may be slowing. Worldwide average annual life expectancy growth was 0.73 percent in the 1960s, and only 3 countries out of the 164 for which we have data saw negative growth. By the 1990s, worldwide average growth had slipped to 0.09 percent, and 36 out of 188 countries saw negative growth. New and reemerging threats—the spread of AIDS, a 65 percent rise in malaria mortality in sub-Saharan Africa between 1970 and 1997—suggest continuing challenges to improvement. This slowing trend of progress, combined with the considerable remaining gaps in performance between developed and developing countries in most areas of quality of life, suggests we may be some considerable distance from global equality in measures of broad-based development. And the global sustainability of progress may be endangered by some of the neo-Malthusian concerns raised at the end of Chapter 4.[23]

A further concern with education statistics in particular is the *quality* of outcomes related to enrollment. Enrollment and learning are two notably different things. For the great majority of the world's primary-age children (around 87 percent of them), the challenge is no longer staying in school but actually learning something while there. A recent survey found that of tested Indian students who had completed the lower primary cycle, 31 percent could not read a simple story and 29 percent could not do two-digit math problems. In Ghana, only one-quarter of fifteen- to nineteen-year-olds scored more than 50 percent on a test of one- and two-digit math questions. There is similar depressing evidence of education quality around the developing world.[24]

Worse, rapid expansion in enrollments often results in further declines in quality, a phenomenon particularly clear in Africa. Malawi's decade-old, underfinanced, and largely unplanned experiment in moving almost overnight to universal primary education is generally regarded as a failure. The number of children in a first-grade class averages one hundred. Four out of ten first-graders repeat the year. Children's achievement scores are among the lowest in Africa. Similarly, according to Michael Clemens of the Center for Global Development, the free primary-schooling initiative launched in Kenya in 2003 saw more than a million additional children showing up for public schooling when the government abolished fees. The explosion in enrollments has put enormous pressure on an already overburdened education system.[25]

Furthermore, the move to free education may have done little to increase total enrollments, merely moving a lot of children from private schools to public schools. All this quite possibly at the cost of average quality, given that privately schooled children in other parts of Africa score better than their publicly schooled counterparts on math and English tests.[26]

Overall, however, the world appears to be a far better place to live in today than it was in the middle of the last century or in any century before that. And life has gotten better in particular for those who suffered the worst living conditions in 1950. This is evidence of considerable success in development. Children born in the developing world today are far more likely to survive to old age than those born fifty years ago. They are far more likely to be educated (and thus literate as adults)—and this is particularly true of girls. They are more likely to enjoy civil and political freedoms. And the gap between the likely fortunes of a child born in the developing world and one born in the developed world has narrowed. In both relative and absolute terms, life in Africa, Asia, Eastern Europe, and Latin America is much better today than it was in the past.

These are not insignificant achievements. Tragedy is not losing a quarter of the value of your 401K in the latest economic downturn. Tragedy is losing your children before they have even gone to school. Every three seconds, a child dies before the age of five in the developing world. But if we had the child mortality rates of a century ago, a child would be dying closer to every second. Again, the ability to read, or security from state violence, is not a minor benefit that pales compared to an extra hundred dollars a year in income.

Income is, in the end, nothing more than a measure of achievement in—and a tool to achieve—a better quality of life. Chapter 6 further discusses the power of income as a measure and a tool in those terms. The great news for global development is that quality of life is (increasingly) cheap.

SIX

THE GREAT NEWS

The Best Things in Life Are Cheap

....

The idea that ever-growing wealth is central to the good life has long been controversial. In *The Wealth of Nations*, Adam Smith argued that escaping poverty only required that people are "tolerably well fed, clothed and lodged." Because of the limited needs of mankind, he felt that the primary purpose of the pursuit of riches in wealthier countries is "regard to the sentiment of mankind . . . to be observed, to be attended to, to be taken notice of."[1] Smith was writing in the late eighteenth century, when GDP per capita in the United Kingdom was somewhere below $1,700. More recently, Nobel winner Amartya Sen has elaborated on the idea of capabilities as better measures of quality of life than mere income. His ideas informed the United Nations Development Program's Human Development Index, an attempt to come up with one number that captures a multi-dimensional view of development progress incorporating health and education.

INCOME MATTERS TO QUALITY OF LIFE

Still, income does matter to the broader quality of life. Rich people can buy more stuff—that is what it is to be rich. Ownership of Hummers and flat-screen TVs and sales of Fiji Water are much higher in Los Angeles than in Lagos. Convergence across countries in the consumption of steak, caviar, and champagne is surely lagging at the least. More important, lack of income is still a barrier to improvement in basic quality of life—health, education, security.

Being poor is undoubtedly bad for your health. Take the case of reproductive health practices among migrant Burmese women on the Thai border. The women are forced migrants, who face continuing poverty, legal discrimination, and limited abortion rights. About half of the deaths of women related to pregnancy are due to botched abortions. Attempts to end an unwanted pregnancy start with comparatively harmless self-medication (using such local remedies as Kathy Pan, a mix of redwood, black pepper, nutmeg, cloves, and sandalwood). But if these homegrown medications fail, the secondary techniques are violent and dangerous. The two most common involve a pummeling vigorous enough to sheer off the placenta and cause uterine rupture (often combined with attempts to pull the fetus out by hand) and "stick abortions," which involve inserting an eight- to ten-centimeter stick into the uterus and leaving it there for days at a time. Prices for such abortion treatments are around one-tenth the cost of an illegal induced abortion performed at a private clinic using modern techniques.[2]

Levels of unwanted pregnancy are connected with a limited demand for contraceptives combined with an uncertain supply. The demand for abortions might be reduced if knowledge and acceptance regarding contraceptive practices spread. And de-

mand for the extreme traditional abortion techniques in particular might be reduced if modern methods were legal and cheap.
But poverty plays its own role here. Traditional approaches are
often the only ones that these migrant women can afford.

Again, the 2000 report from the *Voices of the Poor* project
suggests what the absence of resources for universal coverage
providing the most basic health care meant to one family in
Uganda: Difficulties started in March, when their five-year-old
daughter, Grace, had a serious bout of malaria. Given lack of
money, their first recourse was local herbs. Unfortunately, the
little girl's condition did not improve. The family borrowed some
money and bought a few tablets of chloroquine and aspirin from
the local shop. After some improvement, the girl's health sharply
deteriorated two weeks later. By the beginning of May, Grace
had become very weak. Her parents then sold some chickens
and, with the help of neighbors, took her to Ngora Hospital where
she was immediately admitted. She was seriously anemic and
required an urgent blood transfusion. However, the family was
asked to pay about $5 that they did not have. They went back
home to try and look for money. It was too late. Grace died on
May 8 and was buried the following day.

Beyond the affordability of expensive medical procedures, income allows for easier access to nutrition and preventative health
practices. People living on a dollar a day already spend between
56 and 78 percent of their income on food, leaving little extra to
buy more nutritious fare or even the most basic of preventative
health care services. At the national level, lack of income slows
the rollout of public health measures including sanitation. And
the political economy of public service provision in countries
worldwide means that richer people are more likely to have better access to and quality of service from supposedly "universal"
services where they are available at all. In Africa, for example,

the richest fifth of the population benefits from 30 percent of public health expenditure while the poorest fifth benefits from only 12 percent of such expenditure.[3]

Wealthier countries are, unsurprisingly, healthier, according to a seminal paper by Lant Pritchett and Lawrence Summers. High-income countries see average life expectancies twenty years longer than those in low-income countries. Fewer than 1 percent of children die before the age of five in rich countries compared to 12 percent of children in low-income countries— a comparative toll of 100,000 children dying each year in wealthy countries compared to 10 million in the developing world. Data covering one hundred countries from the year 2000 suggest that variation in income is associated with over 70 percent of the variation in global life expectancies—infant and under-five mortalities, for example. No country with an income per capita above $1,500 has an infant mortality rate above 10 percent. No country with an income per capita above $10,000 sees an infant mortality rate above 2 percent. Again, within countries, evidence from forty-four surveys in twenty-two countries suggests that wealth is significantly correlated with infant and child health— children in richer households are more likely to survive childhood, and adults are more likely to live into old age.[4]

Education is also more easily available to those who can afford the time and resources required for schooling. Poor households face an acute trade-off when it comes to putting their twelve-year-old in school rather than having her work on the family plot or seek some sort of (meagerly) paid employment. Often, they cannot afford the investment in the future that education represents because their consumption needs today are simply too pressing. They may face the cruel choice of reducing their child's future potential by denying her education, or reducing it by denying her adequate nutrition to grow up healthy. Partially as a result, primary-school completion rates average around 74 percent of the potential student body in low-income countries compared to 96 percent in upper-middle-income countries.

Again, wealthy families can purchase security, not least by moving to safer, more expensive neighborhoods—one reason why relatively poor people within countries are far more often the victims of crime. Poor countries are also far more likely to be embroiled in civil war, or subject to invasion. With that comes a greater likelihood for citizens to be attacked, to face famine, or to be forced into flight and refugee status. Civil peace requires stability and a working system of law enforcement, both of which might be considered costly.[5]

Given the obvious links between adequate income and opportunities to reach a decent quality of life covering health, education, and security, it is a simple step to the conventional wisdom that improvements in income play the *predominant* role in improving the education, health, and security of people around the world. Consider, for example, the argument made by development economist Martin Ravallion: "Let us agree that there are dimensions of welfare that cannot be easily aggregated with consumption of market goods—call them 'non-income' dimensions. . . . In practice there is considerable congruence between standard measures for these two dimensions of welfare."[6]

Nonetheless, it is possible to question the central importance of greater income to recent improvements in these areas as well as other measures affecting quality of life. Being poor is bad when you need access to expensive treatments or services. Luckily, however, many of the services and treatments most necessary to increase quality of life are very cheap. A critique of the centrality of income to broader progress in quality of life emphasizes the role of such interventions—vaccines, boiling water, civic organization, basic education. (We will examine these alternate

mechanisms in Chapter 7.) And that is why the evidence suggests only a weak link between income and quality of life over
time.

IS QUALITY OF LIFE GETTING CHEAPER?

Although richer countries and people are, by and large, more
educated, healthier, and more secure than poor countries and
people, there are considerable exceptions to this rule. The Indian
state of Kerala is a well-known example. It has an income per
capita below $300, yet a life expectancy of seventy-two, and only
9 percent of the population is illiterate—far better than a number
of wealthier states and countries. Kerala's life expectancy is the
same as that in Lithuania, which is a member of the European
Union. A state government long committed to broad-based education and health may well have created a virtuous cycle in
quality of life (something we'll explore further in Chapter 7).[7]

At the other end of the scale, the United States, with an income per capita of $29,000 and annual health care expenditure
per head of $5,711, sees a life expectancy of seventy-seven years.
Compare this to Costa Rica, where annual income per head is
$6,500, annual health expenditure per capita is $305, and life expectancy is seventy-nine years. On this measure, Costa Rica provides better health outcomes than the United States on one-fifth
the income and 5 percent of the health budget.

Similarly, people and countries with the same income can see
markedly different outcomes in terms of quality of life. Around
the world, infant mortality rates for those living on a dollar a day
or less vary between under three deaths per hundred infants for
urban Mexico or Nicaragua up to seventeen deaths per hundred
in rural Pakistan. As these cases might suggest, at any particular
household income level it is usually better for your quality of life

to be a relatively poor city dweller in a comparatively developed country than a relatively rich villager in a less developed country. This speaks to the importance of public health interventions and access to ideas. But these cases also suggest that quality of life might be quite cheap—indeed, that it might be getting cheaper.[8]

The United Kingdom reached Vietnam's current average income in the early 1800s. But Vietnam's literacy rate in 2000 was 95 percent compared to 69 percent in the UK in the early 1800s, its life expectancy was sixty-nine years compared to forty-one years in the UK when it had the same income, and its infant mortality was less than one-quarter the UK's in the early 1800s. Indeed, the child mortality level for the very richest of British subjects in the early nineteenth century was three times the *average* rate for Vietnam at the dawn of the twenty-first century.[9]

Or compare Africa to nineteenth-century Europe: In Nigeria in 1995, GDP per head was $1,118. That puts it about equal with Finland's GDP in 1870 ($1,107). But look at education: Nigeria had a literacy rate of 57 percent, compared to Finland's 10 percent rate in 1870. Or life expectancy: Nigeria's 1995 life expectancy was fifty-one years. This figure is higher than that for *any* country in Europe in 1870—better than the UK, which had an income per capita in 1870 approximately three times Nigeria's income in 1995. This is an especially impressive performance given Africa's largely tropical climate, which fosters communicable disease rates far higher than those in Europe.

At the individual as much as the national level, history suggests there is considerably more to quality of life than money. Being very, very rich did not stop Edward VI of England dying of syphilis (or possibly TB), Henry V expiring with a case of dysentery, Queen Mary II passing on from smallpox, or King William III departing with a case of pneumonia. Nor could the mere status of royalty ensure a cure to the fatal food poisoning acquired by Henry I after eating his surfeit of lampreys. And a note to republicans—Oliver Cromwell, despite a combination of absolute power and clean living, died with a case of malaria. Similarly, every modern head of state can surely read, yet Genghis Khan and Charlemagne ruled over considerable empires while illiterate. A number of slaves in the Roman Empire were rich enough to own slaves of their own, and slaves ran the whole bureaucracy of the Ottoman Empire, often living an extremely comfortable lifestyle in the process. Still, money rarely brought them freedom. The power of wealth to make a difference to quality of life depends hugely on the circumstances in which its owners find themselves.

Samuel Preston at the University of Pennsylvania was the first to fully document that quality of life might be getting cheaper over time in the case of health, noting that the life expectancy associated with a given level of income was rising rapidly. Preston himself argued that this global change was three to nine times more important in explaining growth in life expectancy than were changes in income, and we will see evidence to support that view in the rest of this chapter.[10]

Preston compared data on mortality outcomes against data on income for sets of countries over different decades. The results show that the average level of health for a given income per capita improved as each decade passed. For example, at an income of $1,000, expected infant mortality has fallen from twenty per hundred births in 1900 to fourteen per hundred in 1940 and seven per hundred in 2000. This suggests that a country that saw absolutely no income growth over the entire century would still have experienced a nearly two-thirds decline in infant mortality over those one hundred years.[11]

Similarly, countries with a GDP per capita of $300 in 1999 have a predicted life expectancy of forty-six years—the same life expectancy as predicted for a country with an income of $3,000 in 1870. Moreover, countries with a GDP per capita of $3,000 today have almost exactly the same life expectancy as would have been predicted for a country with a GDP per capita of $30,000 in 1870. In other words, the income associated with a given life expectancy has fallen 90 percent over 130 years. The distribution of life expectancy has become far more egalitarian on this measure—yet another sign of the convergence we saw in Chapter 5. In 1870, the predicted life expectancy for a person living in a country with an income of $300 per capita was one-third that for a person living in a country with an income of $30,000 per capita. By 1999, the person in a country with a $300 average income saw a life expectancy more than half as long as in a country one hundred times as rich.[12]

Again, low income appears to have been a shrinking barrier to expanded school enrollment over the past seventy years. In 1930, richer countries saw significantly higher enrollment rates, and the link between wealth and enrollment was strong. By 2000, even very poor countries were seeing high enrollments at low income levels, and the explanatory power of income to predict low or high enrollment had fallen considerably. An analysis of the data suggests that a country with a GDP per capita of $800 in 1930 would typically have a 9 percent primary-school enrollment rate, while a country with the same GDP per capita in 2000 would expect that eighty-four out of every hundred kids would be in school. The evidence for 2000 suggests effectively no relationship between income and enrollment at a GDP per capita of $1,000 or above. A stronger relationship links income and higher levels of education at the secondary and tertiary levels, but even here, the average level of education achieved at a given level of income has increased dramatically over the past fifty years.

The story is similar, if perhaps not so dramatic, with regard to measures of civil and political rights. In 1959, Seymour Martin Lipset's article on the social requisites of democracy established a close link between democracy and income, and this strong link is still apparent. Using data from the Polity measure of civil and political rights (presented in the last chapter), studies have found that wealthier countries seem more likely to have higher Polity scores at any one time. All the same, the same Polity score is associated with lower incomes over time. An income of $1,000 was associated with a Polity score of −2.2 in 1900, compared to -0.1 in 2000.[13]

LIFE DURING GROWTH

That it can be inexpensive to provide a good quality of life, and that the cost is on the decline, helps to explain the weak link between growth in income and improvements in quality of life. Indeed, a number of countries that have seen no recent income growth *at all* have still notched up significant improvements in quality of life. Take a particularly benighted country in economic terms—Haiti. There, income between 1950 and 2002 fell from $1,051 to $752 per capita, while infant mortality more than halved, dropping from 22 percent to 7.8 percent of children under the age of one. Similarly, adult literacy increased from 11 percent to 50 percent, and the country's polity score of political rights increased (if in a somewhat roller-coaster fashion).

The World Bank provides data for twelve countries where income per capita in 2005 was lower than it was in 1960: the Central African Republic, Côte d'Ivoire, Liberia, Madagascar, Nicaragua, Niger, Senegal, Sierra Leone, Venezuela, Zambia, and Zimbabwe, alongside Haiti. Incomes in these twelve countries fell by an average of 27 percent over forty-five years. Over the same period, however, life expectancy in these countries *increased*, by an average of over ten years. Only two of the countries—Zambia and Zimbabwe, both near the epicenter of the global AIDS crisis—saw life expectancies fall. And over the period 1970 to 2000, adult literacy rates increased in every country, close to doubling on average. Among the nine countries for which we have Polity scores regarding civil and political rights in 1960 and 2001, these scores increased in seven out of nine, stayed level in one, and declined in only one.

Regarding health in particular, China provides an example of strong economic growth unassociated with rapid quality-of-life improvement. Mao's Great Leap Forward saw both economic decline and widespread famine. Nonetheless, by the late '60s and '70s, while the economy remained stagnant, life expectancy improved dramatically in rural and urban areas alike. The acceleration in economic growth began after 1980, but since then health status in the country has seen relatively little progress. China saw overall life expectancy growing at 1.6 percent per year in the 1960s and collapsing to around 0.2 percent in the 1980s and 1990s, all while rates of income growth were low before 1980 and high after that.[14]

Joining China in experiencing rapid income growth but sluggish performance in health is Botswana. This country of 1 million has been the star growth performer in Africa over the past thirty years and one of the top economic performers worldwide. Yet it saw the worst performance in life expectancy out of any country on the planet, with an average annual decline of 0.55 percent in 1962–2002, due in large part to the tragedy of the AIDS crisis in the country. Conversely, among the top ten in terms of life expectancy growth over that same period were Gambia, Yemen, Nepal, Bangladesh, and Libya—countries not often associated with stellar income performance.

The relationship between income and health is somewhat stronger when we look at infant and under-five mortality. But still, from 1975 to 2000, 89 percent of the difference across countries in the rate of change in child health has to be explained by something other than different rates of income growth. Furthermore, pretty much everywhere saw improvements in health over the last thirty years. This means that accounting only for the *variation* in health outcomes explains only a part of the *total change* in outcomes. Income, then, can account for considerably less than 11 percent of the total change in infant and under-five mortality across countries between 1975 and 2000 (and even less than that in the case of adult mortality).

A similar story governs education. At any one time, residents of a rich country are more likely to have gone to primary and secondary school and then on to university. They are also more likely to be literate. But it appears that the growth rate of income and the growth rate of school enrollments or literacy outcomes are unrelated across countries. We can tell that it doesn't take income growth to spread educational opportunities because a number of countries too poor to have *ever* seen much income growth have close to universal enrollment levels—countries like Togo, Malawi, Madagascar, Uganda, Rwanda, and Bangladesh. And most of the countries that saw particularly rapid growth in the percentage of children enrolled between 1930 and 2000 are not ones often associated with growth miracles. The countries in which enrollment rates climbed more than fifteen times over those seventy years are Sudan, Vietnam, Liberia, Sierra Leone, Cameroon, Iraq, Iran, Morocco, and (once again) Togo.[15]

Regarding the spread of rights and democracy, MIT economist Daron Acemoglu and his colleagues find that the apparently strong cross-country link between income and measures of democracy at any one point in time disappears when they look at changes in civil and political rights over time. They conclude that "high levels of income per capita do not promote transitions to democracy from non-democracy, nor do they forestall transitions to non-democracy from democracy." Examples abound— the communist bloc collapsed in the 1980s when growth had slowed, not in the 1950s when growth was rapid. India has grown later and more slowly than China, yet was democratic far earlier and remains more democratic to this day. Newly independent African states moved toward autocracy in the 1960s and 1970s, a period of comparatively successful economic performance. They moved back toward democracy in the 1980s and 1990s, when growth was markedly slower.[16]

Across countries, if we look at cases where there was declining income over a twenty-year period during the last century, Polity scores in these 65 cases increased by an average of 4.11, compared to an average increase of 1.69 in the 310 cases where country income growth was positive. If anything, then, income collapse is far more associated with democratization than is income growth.[17]

Regarding violence, wealthy countries appear to be less often victim to civil war, less often perpetrators of mass killings of civilians, and less likely to fight one another. Think of Thomas Friedman's Golden Arches Theory of international relations—that (Serbia and NATO aside) no two countries with a McDonald's have gone to war. But at the same time, the number of major wars ongoing worldwide rose from four to twenty-six between 1946 and 1991, before dropping back to five by 2005. This suggests a close association with the course of the Cold War and democratization rather than with income growth and consumption of Happy Meals. And, indeed, cross-country studies suggest that income growth does not reduce the chance that a country will become embroiled in civil war, either.[18]

Regarding crime, poor people are more likely to be victims, and poor women in particular are more likely to be victims of domestic violence. Yet global evidence on homicide and robbery rates suggests that while levels of crime across countries are connected with both inequality and recent economic downturns, they are not closely associated with the level of GDP per capita, let alone long-term trends in growth. The murder rate in the Caribbean is more than three times that in East Africa, for example. And again, (poor) India and (rich) Japan share very low rates of violent crime. Only around 1 percent of people were threatened with violence or attacked in the period 2000–2005 in either country. Countries with incomes around or between Indian and Japanese levels, including the United States, South Africa, and Brazil, saw far higher rates of violence. Between 12 and 20 percent of people were threatened or attacked over the same five-year period in those countries.[19]

Looking at a wider range of measures, economist Bill Easterly explored "Life During Growth" and discovered that the rate of improvement in almost all of the quality-of-life indicators that he studied was only weakly related to the rate of economic growth. Overall, Easterly's study found that for only eight of sixty-nine indicators was there any statistically significant positive relationship between income and change in quality of life—being richer doesn't necessarily equate with higher quality of life. And his study suggested that income change was a driving factor behind improvements in only three measures of quality of life: calorie intake, protein intake, and fixed-line telephones per capita. It was not a significant cause, not strongly related or negatively related to another sixty-six measures covering life expectancy and health, quality of government, political instability, education, transport and communication, and environmental quality. Again, while rich countries have more doctors and nurses per capita, more access to clean water, more education, fewer war deaths, better human rights, and the like, *growth* of income over the last thirty years is not strongly related to the speed of improvement in any of these indicators of quality of life. At the same time, countries that grow faster *do* see more manslaughter and carbon dioxide emissions.[20]

This weak link between improvements in quality of life and income growth may help to account for one more oft-noted weak relationship—that between GDP per capita growth and "subjective happiness." Happiness surveys ask people questions along the lines of "Taking your life as a whole, do you consider yourself not very happy, somewhat happy, or very happy?" Poll responses tend to be related to respondents' degree of happiness as viewed by friends and family, to how often they smile, and even to levels of chemicals in the bloodstream that doctors associate with "happy feelings." Such responses are lower among groups you'd expect to be less happy: the unemployed, prisoners, the recently divorced, and the recently injured.

The good news is that, over time, we have also seen some increase in subjective happiness levels across developing countries. But those countries that have experienced considerable GDP per capita growth have not seen more rapid increases in subjective well-being. Reducing unemployment, increasing the availability of marriage counseling services, and creating more prison furlough programs might therefore be better policy responses to maximizing happiness than fostering GDP growth.[21]

A WEAK RELATIONSHIP—OR JUST BAD DATA?

The relationship between income growth and improvements in quality of life could be stronger than it appears in this initial look at the evidence. Not least, we've seen that there are significant

concerns with the quality of data. But these are mitigated somewhat by the fact that across a whole range of different quality-
of-life measures (and different measures of income), and over
periods as long as a century, when there have been very large
changes in both income and quality of life, we *continually* get
the same result. The weakness of the relationship also holds when
we use only more recent, higher-quality survey data.[22]

Perhaps there are significant lags between increases in income
and improvements in quality of life, with advances in income
taking years to have an effect. There is considerable historical
evidence from now-wealthy countries that life expectancy is far
more sensitive to income (and income growth) at birth and in
early childhood than it is to changes in income later at life, for
example.[23] This finding is supported by somewhat stronger evidence of the link between contemporaneous child health and
income than of the link between overall life expectancy and
health that we saw above.

At the same time, even quite significant delayed effects on life
expectancy based on a larger impact of income growth in early
life would be picked up at least in the analysis of income and
health growth over periods as long as a century (which covers
three to five generations). And we've seen that century-long relationships remain weak. Once again, as Lant Pritchett notes,
many countries in Africa have *never* seen significant economic
growth; their income today is just too low to suggest that they
were ever much poorer in the past.[24] If much of the region has
seen broadly stagnant incomes since the birth of civilization, it
can't be that income growth some time ago accounts for improved health in Africa today. We have also seen cases from
around the world where incomes have been stagnant for forty
years and yet health, education, and rights have all dramatically
improved.

We might expect to see a declining health return to each additional dollar of income. People living on a dollar a day spend somewhere around four-fifths of their resources on food, and yet many are still malnourished. If their income dropped much further, they would starve. Those living on, say, one hundred times that income can already afford considerable and advanced medical care alongside better sanitation and a safer household environment. There are even concerns that, above a certain level, the health returns to greater income may turn negative thanks to excessive consumption.[25]

So, adding an extra dollar a day to the income of someone living in absolute poverty would surely be associated with a larger health impact than adding a dollar a day to someone already living on $30,000 a year. And Preston's findings on health, mirrored by a similar pattern in education, do suggest that the improvement in quality of life associated with each dollar of additional income declines the richer a country becomes.[26] It may be, then, that there is a strong impact of GDP per capita growth on quality of life at low incomes, which diminishes as countries become richer. Is it this possibility alone that clouds a strong cross-country relationship between income and quality of life?[27]

The short answer is "no." We've seen that even without *any* increase at all in GDP per capita, significant improvements in quality of life can be—and frequently have been—accomplished. Perhaps unsurprisingly, even if we restrict an analysis of income growth and quality-of-life improvement to poor countries, relationships still appear weak.[28]

On the other hand, it is worth noting that the relationships we do see between income and quality of life might be because better quality of life raises incomes rather than (or as well as) because incomes raise quality of life. That's obvious in the case of education, where increased "human capital" is a staple of growth theories, as we have seen. But there is also a considerable literature linking improved health causally to income, for example. This makes intuitive sense. Healthy workers can work harder, healthy kids can learn better. Parents who can be reasonably confident that their kids will survive to adulthood might decide to have fewer children and, as a result, be able to invest more in the quality of life of those children they do have. David Weil at Brown University recently reviewed numerous studies suggesting that adequate nutrition and good health are strongly associated with subsequent productivity and income at both the individual and national levels. He provides an estimate suggesting that health can account for between 10 and 23 percent of the global variation in income per capita. And some evidence suggests that liberty and civil peace are also potential sources of long-run income growth.

Of course, Chapter 3 suggested some reasons to doubt that education and health were really that central to the medium-run growth story. But it is at least as plausible to imagine that improvements in health, education, and civil and political rights account for what relationship we do see between them and income growth—rather than the other way around.[29]

THE PRICE OF THE GOOD LIFE

It used to take some fair income at the country level to guarantee health, to provide education, perhaps even to ensure freedoms. It now costs less. New inventions in the case of health, as well as new ideas and conceptions in the case of education and freedoms, mean that at lower cost you can get the same outcome. Take Vietnam, a country with a 2003 GDP per capita of $2,147, which placed it firmly in the low-income-country category and the bottom quarter of global country incomes. We have seen that its people had an average life expectancy of nearly seventy—three score years and ten. Around 2 percent of infants died in their first year. Vietnam had a literacy rate of above 90 percent and close to universal primary-school completion.

These figures are all considerably better than those for the UK when it had a similar income. A national income of perhaps $2,000 per capita today, if well spent, is enough to provide for many elements of the good life. This was not the case in the 1800s. Back then, an income of more than $2,000 *mattered*. It led to considerably lower infant mortality and so on. The success of development has been to reduce the cost and to spread the reach of the good life.

While income remains important especially in the world's poorest countries, over the longer term even complete income stagnation has not considerably slowed improvements in a range of measures of quality of life. Paul Collier has argued persuasively that the "Bottom Billion" of the world's population is stuck in dysfunctional economies that struggle to escape the poverty trap.[30] The good news is that even most of the Bottom Billion have seen plenty of progress in health, education, and rights over the past forty years—there is scant evidence of a quality-of-life trap.

Rich countries have led the way in developing some of the global technologies that have helped lower the cost of quality of life, of course. And yet it is clear that the most important technological advances in this regard did not require particle accelerators, Hubble telescopes, or other billion-dollar research adventures to uncover. Not every country needs to become rich if the goal is (only) to achieve some minimum level of quality of life worldwide. And existing resources could be far better utilized if the aim is to maximize improvements in the global quality of life going forward.

Further good news is that if large incomes are less and less requisite to ensuring a good quality of life, so are the consumption patterns of wealthy countries and their associated environmental costs. One of the few outcomes strongly associated with income growth that Bill Easterly found in his study of "Life During Growth" was rising output of various pollutants. But levels of output that are sustainable from the point of view of the global environment can support a growing number of people at a higher quality of life over time. To ensure universal education and low child mortality, the whole world needn't be rich enough to buy thirty items a week off the Home Shopping Network.

Chapter 7 examines what lies behind the phenomenon of the cheaper quality of life. In earlier chapters we saw that the technologies that matter for economic growth are process technologies. In the next chapter we will see that for health, both ideas and invented technologies (boiling water to kill germs, vaccinations) are perhaps the key to improved outcomes. We'll also see that ideas, supported to a lesser extent by invented technologies including communications, may be central to other elements of quality of life including education and civil rights.

SEVEN

DRIVERS OF THE BETTER LIFE

Innovation and Ideas

....

I n 1938, a biological expedition sponsored by the American Museum of Natural History arrived in West New Guinea. Expedition leader Richard Archbold was to survey the area by seaplane, in the first such attempt. His second survey mission took place on June 23, when, after hours of flying over near-impenetrable jungle, his plane passed over the Grand Valley of the Balim River. The valley was occupied by fifty thousand Papuans, until that point unknown to—and unknowing of—the outside world. After six weeks of ferrying men and equipment to the nearest landing point for his seaplane, patrols from the Archbold expedition met with the inhabitants of the Grand Valley. This meeting was the last (substantial) first contact in history.[1]

At the time of first contact, the West Papuans were living a Stone Age existence. Early estimates of infant mortality were as high as 20 or 30 percent. Children stunted by the effects of malnutrition were the norm. Despite high child mortality rates from natural causes, techniques including female infanticide and the killing of twins were commonly practiced, and when these failed, warfare and cannibalism stalked in the rear (as Malthus might have it). Casualties from war accounted for as much as 10 to 30 percent of all male deaths.[2]

Integration with the rest of the world certainly carried costs to West Papuans. Not least, their unique culture and language have continued to pass away. The spread of imported disease led to epidemics of influenza and dysentery in the 1940s. And the political situation in the region (where there is a strong independence movement and a history of repression) involves considerable constraints on civil and political rights. On the other hand, overall levels of violence have decreased markedly, and the long-term trend has been toward considerably improved health and improved access to education. While infant mortality in West Papua remains as high as 9 to 15 percent, this is likely one-half of the precontact level. The region's encounter with the "global technological frontier" has ultimately been a force for improved quality of life.[3]

What is true for West Papua is also true for the rest of the "New" World. First contact with the people of the Europe-Asia-Africa landmass carried considerable short-term costs, not least in terms of disease. But over the long term, the interconnections among the global population—to a greater or lesser degree—have been a powerful force for the spread of technologies and ideas that have improved quality of life worldwide. Indeed, people as poor as their forebears were when they encountered the global technology frontier are benefiting almost as much as those who have grown far richer over time.

GLOBAL PATTERNS OF CHANGE IN QUALITY OF LIFE

There is a strong pattern of change to global outcomes in health that is common across countries. Compared to this global pattern, different rates of economic growth, or health financing, or education rates, or policy choices—or war, famine, or plague—across countries play a limited role in explaining changes in health over time. For example, all country-specific factors added together can account for only about one-seventh of the average change in infant mortality across the sixty-eight countries for which we have data between 1950 and 2000. The other six-sevenths of mortality change in these countries can be better accounted for by the global pattern of decline.[4]

Related to the finding of similar rates of progress over the long term around the world is that variations from this trend rate of progress tend to be short-lived. As they say on mutual fund prospectuses, past performance is no guarantee of future results. Relatively strong performance in improving health today is absolutely no guarantee of strong relative performance tomorrow. If anything, strong performance one decade is associated with somewhat *weaker* performance the next—there is reversion over time toward the average rate of global change.[5]

A similar finding of a strong global pattern of change applies to other aspects of quality of life. With regard to developments in education, Michael Clemens describes an s-curve of progress that applies to primary-school attendance across countries and time. Slow initial progress in expanding enrollments from very low levels in the first thirty years of the transition toward universal education is followed by rapid enrollment growth toward ubiquity. Progress slows once again as countries reach toward 100 percent enrollment rates. This transition suggests that a country that reaches 50 percent of primary-age kids enrolled today will reach 70 percent enrollment after twenty-two years and 90 percent after fifty-eight years. Around 90 percent of the variation in net primary enrollment in all countries for the postwar period can be accounted for by this common global pattern of transition, argues Clemens.[6]

Again, Daron Acemoglu and his colleagues found a global pattern of transition when they looked at the trend toward greater respect for civil rights and democracy worldwide. And Bill Easterly's study of seventy different measures of quality of life covering health, education, rights, the environment, and access to infrastructure found that a global pattern was a driving explanatory factor for progress in nearly all of them over the past thirty years.[7] Of course, there are exceptions—AIDS and civil war can stall and even temporarily reverse progress on health, and have done so. The fall of the Berlin Wall considerably accelerated progress toward greater respect for civil and political rights. Nonetheless, the transition to a higher quality of life overall follows a similar pattern across measures and countries alike.

The apparent importance of processes that are broadly common across countries—whatever their economic performance, policy behavior, or institutional development—suggests conclusions about the role of governments or country circumstances in speeding or retarding progress on quality of life. All countries have moved toward a greater government role in the provision of quality of life, suggesting that government actions may play a part in explaining the global rate of quality-of-life change. At the same time, the common transition pattern implies that there must be an upper limit to the importance not only of different rates of income growth but also of different speeds of policy or institutional change in explaining relatively fast or slow progress in quality of life over time across countries.

A model of development that suggests a strong influence of factors common across countries, that predicts convergence of outcomes, and that sees a comparatively minor role for policy differences across countries in explaining variation in outcomes is Robert Solow's "exogenous growth model" discussed in Chapter

3. We saw that it was abandoned by analysts of economic growth as singularly failing to account for changes in GDP per capita across countries over time. But the model fits far better with the facts of global change in other measures of quality of life where change *does* appear to be driven by strong global trends and countries further behind *are* rapidly catching up. In turn, this suggests that the factors that drive the exogenous model—the global diffusion of technology and ideas—might play a larger role in quality-of-life outcomes than they appear to have with income growth.

THE SPREAD OF TECHNOLOGIES

We have seen that the hope and expectation of early economic growth models was that the technology behind growth would flow to seek a common level—like water. Technology would spread without regard to distance and borders, ending up about the same everywhere. The medieval would not cohabit with the modern. In turn, this would create a powerful force for income convergence.

Again, we've seen that hope was optimistic. The process technologies—institutions like laws and inventory management systems—that appear central to raising incomes per capita flow less like water and more like bricks. But ideas and inventions— the importance of ABCs and vaccines for DPT—really might flow more easily across borders and over distances. Or at least they might flow with somewhat less regard to local idiosyncrasies and customs. They may be a little more like water—or at least Jell-O—than like bricks. Such technologies and ideas, we have already seen, may be central to allowing more people to live at the same income in the same country (thereby overcoming the Malthusian trap). And they may also be the central force behind improvements in broader quality of life worldwide, even in places that have seen little or no income growth.

Consider again the comparison of Vietnam today with the UK in the early 1800s. While the two countries had similar incomes per capita, people in the UK in the past had far less choice in things to buy than a modern Vietnamese person living on the same income. The British subject in 1815 could rarely refrigerate foods, light the house after dark, or keep in instant contact with friends and family over long distances. Vietnamese people living on the same income today are considerably richer in that their choice of goods and services to purchase is much greater—they can buy vaccines, refrigerated foods, lightbulbs, or telephone calls. They are also richer in that they have far better information on which to base their choices—regarding hand washing, or what to do to help their child with diarrhea, for example.

Again, while poor Indians may have an income similar to that of the medieval Briton (as we saw in Chapter 2), they also live longer, are far more likely to be literate, and have considerably more rights. This is in large part because they have access to a stock of technology and ideas that would have been considered magical or heretical in 1500. For example, nearly one out of every six of the poorest Indians had electric lighting. And while some Indian cultures still leave considerable room for discrimination against women and untouchables, the legal system largely combats rather than upholds such behavior.

The range of technologies that are available and utilized by many of the world's poorest people today but were far less ubiquitous fifty or a hundred years ago is considerable. Beyond medical technologies including bed nets, vaccination, and antibiotics, the list would include building materials such as cement, corrugated iron, steel wire, piping, nails, and tools; household items including plastic sheeting and containers; synthetic and cheap cotton clothing; transport technologies from rubber soles to bicycles; infrastructure services including all-weather roads and buses; water pumps, radios, televisions, mobile phones, and butane and paraffin for lighting; and pens, papers, and books. On the side of ideas, the germ theory and its implications, the concept of democracy, and the value of education for boys and girls alike have gained considerably greater acceptance in countries rich and poor. These technologies and ideas have had a considerable impact on a range of measures of quality of life, and they have spread worldwide.

The comparatively easy flow of innovations central to quality of life helps to account for the considerable evidence of strong global patterns of change in terms of quality of life. It also might help to explain the process of global quality-of-life convergence even without income convergence—and the improvements in health and education in Africa even absent any substantive income growth at all.

THE SPREAD OF HEALTHY EATING

A major set of technologies that have spread across much of the world are improved crop varieties. These are a vital factor behind the global escape from the Malthusian trap discussed in Chapter 4. And the fact that adequate nutrition is now more widespread and affordable is also an important cause of longer life expectancy in the developing world.

Average global food supplies per person increased by about a quarter between 1961 and 1999, with a more rapid increase in developing countries. The proportion of the world's population living in countries where per capita food supplies were under 2,200 calories per day was 56 percent in the mid-1960s, compared to below 10 percent by the 1990s. Sub-Saharan Africa did

lag on this indicator, with per capita food supplies increasing
only 6 percent between 1961 and 1999. On the other hand, in
1999 this still put sub-Saharan Africa's average daily food supply
14 percent higher than the *average* for developing countries in
1961.[8]

Again, food prices declined by approximately one-half in the
second fifty years of the twentieth century alone. The Green Revolution of improved agricultural productivity has played a dramatic role in reducing the cost of life and decreasing the threat
of widespread famine. Recent price increases temporarily eroded
some of this gain; nonetheless, it is worth noting that adequate
calorific supply has been available at such low incomes that obe-
sity is becoming a global epidemic. We've seen that, worldwide,
there are as many people overweight as malnourished and that
300 million of the overweight classify as obese.[9]

SEWAGE, CITIES, AND DISEASE

Even at the same level of average calorie consumption per capita,
we have seen dramatic improvements in health outcomes. In
1940, a country with an income per capita (not adjusted for purchasing power) between $150 and $299 and an average daily
calorie consumption of below 2,100 would have a predicted life
expectancy of around thirty-six years. By 1970, this had increased
to fifty-two years. The story spreads far beyond improved nutrition to encompass a range of health technologies.[10]

We can illustrate the growing importance of increasingly cheap
inventions and ideas to health outcomes by looking at the history of waterborne disease. Rapid urbanization during the Industrial Revolution in Europe was accompanied by downturns
in health linked to increased disease exposure. This was, not
least, because of appallingly inadequate sanitation. Writers at

the time describe huge piles of human and animal excrement collecting in the streets and fetid rivers almost solid with waste. Because of these health risks, urban life expectancy remained considerably below rural life expectancy throughout the nineteenth century.[11]

Cholera was one significant cause of this health imbalance. The bacteria spread through contaminated water and produce a toxin in the small intestine that leads to spasms and abdominal pains, vomiting, and—most deadly—gushing diarrhea. This highly infectious liquid is the usual source of transmission—contaminating water supplies and reaching new hosts. Cholera outbreaks were a regular feature of nineteenth-century urban living worldwide—one attack in 1849 took more than 14,000 lives in London alone.

Public health measures including large-scale sewage systems eventually played a role in arresting the urban health decline in the middle of the century. These were some of the most complex and expensive public works projects undertaken at the time. Nonetheless, early sewage systems were constructed before anyone had discovered the real reason they might help reduce disease. Indeed, London's early systems made things worse, not better, by dumping the raw sewage in the Thames some distance upstream of intake pipes for many of the city's water companies. Sadly, the systems were built on the theory it was the stench—"miasma"—that was responsible for illnesses such as cholera. So long as the smell was limited to the river, so the thinking went, no harm was done.

John Snow's analysis of London's cholera outbreaks in the 1850s formed the scientific basis for overturning miasma theories and connecting the disease with infected water. A further spur to sewage reform was Pasteur's early work confirming the germ theory of disease. And with the 1865 completion of Joseph

Bazalgette's five new sewer lines that transported waste to the east out of the city, the capital freed itself from major cholera outbreaks—if at considerable expense.[12]

The germ theory took some time to gain acceptance worldwide. Indeed, we'll see that many in the developing world are not aware of the theory to this day. But once the theory did spread and disease became better understood, more cost-effective interventions than networked water became available to reduce the burden of waterborne illness. Well-designed pit latrines can protect people at much lower cost than networked sewage systems, and with similar efficacy. Programs to encourage householders to add a small amount of bleach to drinking water in developing countries have reduced diarrhea cases by 50 to over 80 percent.[13]

And as well as reducing the risk of contamination, we have learned some cheap cures. For example, oral rehydration—using a combination of sugar and salt dissolved in water—can effectively treat cholera and prevent deaths from other causes of diarrhea. As a result, cholera and in particular cholera deaths are increasingly rare worldwide. An exceptional outbreak in Zimbabwe that took the lives of over 4,000 people in 2008–2009 is a sign of how far Robert Mugabe's regime had driven public health provision into the ground.

As knowledge of cheap sanitation and treatment techniques has spread around the globe, the impact of piped water and sanitation access on health outcomes has declined, while the role of education has grown. This to the extent that one multicountry study of child mortality in the developing world suggested that universal access to improved water and sanitation would reduce global child mortality rates by as little as 3 percent.[14]

As knowledge has become key to health, it appears that the advantages of living in an urban area now considerably outweigh the disadvantages. Being in an environment where traditional approaches are more easily abandoned, ideas can spread rapidly, and access to new technologies such as antibiotics is more straightforward outweighs the health costs of crowded living in unsanitary conditions. This is why the urban-rural health gradient has reversed worldwide. Infant mortality in cities with a population of above 1 million is almost one-half the rural rate in Asia, and around a third lower in Africa, the Middle East, and Latin America. And the urban advantage holds even in places with limited sanitation—in sub-Saharan Africa only a little more than half of the urban population has access to improved sanitation, for example.[15]

The declining importance of expensive interventions like networked sanitation to outcomes is also reflected in a declining relationship between growth in incomes and improvements in health around the world. Historical data on income and health suggest that between 1820 and 1910, when life expectancy depended on knowledge and capacities available only to the wealthy and then on expensive and complex public works, countries and regions that saw faster economic growth also saw more rapid improvements in health. But in the twentieth century, when life expectancy depended increasingly on the supply of and demand for cheap technologies, we saw the income-health relationship break down, even among poor economies.[16]

GOOD HEALTH NEED NOT BE EXPENSIVE

Through a range of technologies and approaches it has thus become possible to provide increasingly improved health outcomes at low and declining cost. A particularly dramatic example involves the global eradication of smallpox.

Smallpox symptoms begin with headache, fever, pains, and vomiting. Three to five days later, the skin begins to erupt in pustules. Bacteria often contaminate these pustules, leading to abscesses, septic joints, or corneal ulcers that in turn can lead to blindness. Between 15 and 45 percent of victims eventually perish—in many cases as a result of septic shock.

Smallpox has been one of the world's greatest killers. Around 3.5 million Aztec Indians died of the disease after it was introduced by Spanish conquistadors. In Europe at the end of the eighteenth century, the disease was killing 400,000 each year. Dr. Edward Jenner introduced smallpox vaccination in 1796, and yet deaths continued worldwide—including that of China's Tongzhi Emperor, as we saw in Chapter 5. Over the course of the twentieth century, smallpox was still responsible for a total of between 300 million and 500 million deaths.

In 1959, the World Health Assembly adopted the global eradication of smallpox as a goal. And in 1966, a budget of $2.5 million was provided to the World Health Organization to coordinate the global eradication program and provide assistance to countries where smallpox was still endemic. These countries had a combined population of over 1 billion, suggesting a per capita expenditure of one-quarter of one cent that year—although this amount did not include the cost of the vaccines themselves, which were donated by member-countries. Over the course of the next ten years, the number of countries with cases of smallpox dropped from forty-six to none.

The total cost of the program over those ten years (including donor and endemic country expenditure) was in the region of $312 million—perhaps 32 cents per person in infected countries. The eradication program cost about the same as producing five recent Hollywood blockbusters, or the wing of a B-2 bomber, or a little under one-tenth the cost of Boston's recent road-improvement project nicknamed the Big Dig. However much one admires the improved views of the Boston waterfront, the lines of the stealth bomber, or the acting skills of Keira Knightley in *Pirates of the Caribbean*, or indeed of the gorilla in *King Kong*, this still seems like a very good deal.[17]

The eradication of smallpox was an easy task compared to the complexities of eradicating malaria or AIDS. The disease attached no stigma, it had no animal reservoir, it did not rapidly mutate, it had early and visible symptoms, and its host either was rapidly killed or recovered with immunity. Furthermore, the vaccine was cheap, stable, long lasting, and easy to administer (a person trained for one hour can vaccinate 1,500 people a day). Yet the complete eradication of what was once a major killer was achieved in countries rich and poor, some at war or in civil strife, many with failing health institutions and decaying infrastructure.

The low cost and global success of the smallpox eradication program suggest the power of ideas and technologies to dramatically improve quality-of-life outcomes even in the very worst of settings—and even where incomes are stagnant. And smallpox eradication does not look like it will be a one-off victory. For example, polio is now endemic in only four countries, and the disease's death toll has fallen from a thousand a day to below a thousand a year.

The global decline in mortality over the past sixty years is significantly linked to the spread of a range of such cheap technologies—the yellow fever vaccine in the 1940s, antibiotics by the early 1950s, the use of DDT to spray houses in the 1940s and '50s, and, more recently, a number of newer vaccines. There has been a rapid convergence in the use of such technologies around the world. Between 1974 and 2000, with the support of the United Nations' Expanded Program on Immunization, the immunization rate for six diseases—measles, diphtheria, pertussis, tetanus, tuberculosis, and polio—increased from 5 to 80 percent of the

world's newborns. Between 1975 and 2000, this growing worldwide immunization rate alone could account for a considerable
proportion of global average improvement in child health. Between 1999 and 2005, thanks to the continued rollout of vaccinations, the number of African children who died annually from
measles dropped by three-quarters from over a half-million to
around 126,000.[18]

Vaccines are one example of a general rule: The most effective
health technologies are very cheap and very simple. The Bellagio
Child Survival Study Group, a team of medical experts assem-
bled by the leading British medical journal *The Lancet* in 2003,
concluded that fully one-third of the 10 million child deaths in
low-income countries that still occur each year could be prevented through the use of oral rehydration therapy, breast feeding, and insecticide-treated bed nets. Bed nets cost around $5.
Oral rehydration therapy involves a simple solution of sugar and
salt in water. Breast feeding takes time and maternal nutrition,
but otherwise it is free—and certainly considerably cheaper than
baby formula.[19]

Again, the most effective health-sector interventions do not
need to involve hospitals or doctors. For example, Malaysia and
Sri Lanka have both made competent, professional midwives
available in rural areas in addition to ensuring access to drugs
and equipment. As a result, since the 1930s the rate of maternal
deaths during childbirth has dropped by 98 percent in Malaysia
and by 99 percent in Sri Lanka. Current mortality levels are only
marginally higher than in the United States. Yet expenditure on
maternal and child health services in Sri Lanka and Malaysia is
below 0.4 percent of GDP. The cost of a basic package of primary
health services in rural areas ranged from around US$3 per head
per year in Cambodia to US$6 per head per year in Guatemala,

according to a recent survey. In all cases studied, the amounts represent less than 1 percent of income per capita.[20]

At the other end of the scale, direct measures of comparably expensive and institutionally demanding health inputs—such as hospital beds or doctors—do not appear to be strongly associated with health outcomes. The ratio of hospital beds to populations has declined around the world since 1960, from 4.2 per thousand people to 3.0 per thousand in 2005—this over a period when global health has improved at historically unprecedented rates. And changes in the number of doctors, nurses, and hospital beds per capita are not significantly related to changes in infant or child mortality across countries. Even access to health clinics in developing countries appears to have a fairly limited impact on health outcomes. This is not to say that hospital care is irrelevant to health—doctors and surgeons save and improve many thousands of lives every day. It is merely to suggest that their efficacy is limited when compared to preventative and basic care, which can save many millions.[21]

In turn, these outcomes help to account for the numerous studies that have found no link at all between overall health expenditures and health outcomes in countries rich and poor alike. We saw in Chapter 6 that Costa Rica spends 5 percent of what the United States spends on health per person, but the average Costa Rican lives two years longer. In Vietnam, where life expectancy has reached seventy years, health expenditure per capita per year is only $23. That is 0.4 percent of the US expenditure for 91 percent of the life expectancy.[22]

Similarly, the importance of widespread basic care over focused advanced care to outcomes is clear from China's recent health trajectory, which we have seen does not match its impressive performance on measures of income. Per capita health spending increased seven-fold in the rural areas of China between 1990 and 2002, but rural health has stagnated. One factor may be the collapse of the Cooperative Medical System of insurance, which provided basic care for 90 percent of the rural population in the late 1970s. The system fell apart after agriculture-sector reform and a 65 percent decline in government subsidies. By 1993, only 21 percent of China's population had insurance. The number of active primary health care workers in rural areas declined 36 percent 1980–1989. And the efficacy of care provided to those still lucky enough to have coverage has fallen. A survey of health centers and village clinics in areas of Chongqing and Gansu in China concluded that less than 2 percent of drug prescriptions were reasonable given best-practice standards and that there is growing evidence of the overuse of surgery. Both of these developments were in part driven by the financial incentives doctors and clinics face under the new health services regime. A system that once provided near-universal access to basic care now provides limited coverage that extends to expensive, often unnecessary, medical techniques—all at seven times the price.[23]

THE DEMAND SIDE OF HEALTH

If cheap and simple health technologies that don't require access to hospitals or doctors are available that could dramatically improve global health, why isn't everyone already using them? For some interventions, there are still significant issues of supply— vaccines not available, midwives not trained—and this is a topic we will return to. But supply issues are comparatively minor for many of the most cost-effective approaches. Breast feeding, hand washing, and sugar-salt solutions don't take an advanced health service to deliver. Instead, it is the demand side that matters. A major reason behind poor health in developing countries is that people are not using available technologies, through lack of knowledge or incentives.

In India, the percentage of parents who think the correct treatment for a child with diarrhea is to reduce the amount they are given to drink (absolutely the wrong thing to do) varies considerably from state to state. Fewer than 5 percent give this wrong answer in states like Kerala, where we have seen that health outcomes are very strong. Above 50 percent suggest this response in West Bengal—where child mortality in the 1990s was about three times as high as in Kerala.[24]

Again, we have seen that the germ theory of disease has been central to the development and spread of numerous health-saving interventions as powerful yet mundane as hand washing. But only one-third of respondents in a Ghanaian survey understood that ill health related to sanitation was the result of germs rather than heat, smell, or dirt, for example. In rural Guinea-Bissau, only 16 percent of interviewed parents had heard of pneumonia, even though it is responsible for as many as one-third of child deaths in the country.[25]

Evidence from household survey data covering 278,000 children across forty-five developing countries supports the importance of the demand side of health. This evidence, compiled by Peter Boone of the London School of Economics and Zhaoguo Zhan of Brown University, suggests that the prevalence of common diseases that kill children has little predictive power for child mortality. Instead, actions taken by parents to help sick children are the most significant factors determining differences in child survival. Boone and Zhan estimated that improvements in treatment-seeking and education among parents might reduce child mortality by roughly 32 percent. Mirroring the results from Indian states is the fact that, across the same forty-five countries, children whose mothers believed fluids should be reduced during diarrhea episodes faced a 15 percent greater risk of death than children whose mothers were better informed. Educated parents exposed to the media, as well as those living in communities where others knew the correct response, were also more likely to know how to treat diarrhea events and thereby save lives. Once knowledge and education were taken into account, household income played a marginal role in determining health outcomes for the quarter-million-plus children across the forty-five countries in the study.[26]

Educated mothers in particular are better informed about and more likely to use a range of health facilities and medical technologies. For example, they are more likely to have their children immunized, to have received prenatal care, and to have their deliveries attended by trained personnel. In Mali in 1995 more than a quarter of children born to mothers with no education died before the age of five as compared to one in ten whose mothers had secondary education.[27]

That demand matters and is linked to education in particular suggests a role for an adoption curve regarding new health technologies, with educated people more likely to be first adopters while the illiterate catch up over time. (Meanwhile, the educated are adopting the next innovation in turn.) Survey evidence supports such a process of adoption by example, as we saw above: People in communities where general uptake of health services is low are less likely to seek such services themselves.

Cultural factors may also play a role in determining who are the first beneficiaries of health knowledge and information-improved practices. In India, scheduled castes (such as the untouchables) are considerably less likely to seek immunization and antenatal services for their children, regardless of how rich they are. Also in India, mothers wean girls more rapidly than boys, in part to overcome the contraceptive properties of nursing and so increase the chance of conceiving a son in the near future. Seema Jayachandran and Ilyana Kuziemko estimate that this early weaning helps account for higher female child mortality—with about 22,000 additional Indian girls dying each year.[28]

Adding to evidence that the demand side is at work, a number of studies confirm the importance of demand-stimulation as an effective tool. Conditional cash transfers pay recipients to use health or education facilities, for example. Such programs have had considerable impact on clinic attendance, treatment completion rates, and health outcomes, discussed at greater length in the next chapter. In many cases, the impact of the transfers persists after payments end, suggesting that payments foster changes in attitudes. Social marketing—fostering socially beneficial behavioral change using the same Madison Avenue techniques used to create demand for cars or musical air fresheners—also has a record of considerable success. Once again, we'll look at examples in the next chapter.[29]

Finally, health education programs have also seen strong returns. An evaluation of a maternal and child health program including door-to-door delivery of advice and immunization in Matlab, a rural area of Bangladesh, found that the program significantly reduced gender and socioeconomic differences in immunization take-up. This was in considerable part due to the fact that mothers under the program had a better perception of the risks of leaving their children unvaccinated. In the slums of Karachi, a randomized trial found that education regarding improved hygiene combined with soap distribution reduced respiratory infections by 50 percent and diarrhea by 53 percent.[30]

THE DIFFUSION OF EDUCATION

A similar set of findings regarding the importance of ideas applies to the spread of education. We've seen evidence of dramatic global progress, suggesting that universal basic education appears to be an affordable benefit at very low levels of income. The speed of expansion in primary and secondary enrollments over the last thirty years is largely unconnected with the rate of GDP per capita growth or (to any great degree) other policy or institutional changes at the country level. And again, the demand side appears to have become the predominant factor in determining education outcomes.[31]

Michael Clemens, who estimated the speed of transition to universal education, does suggest that the transition path after World War II has been a little steeper than that in the later nineteenth and early twentieth centuries. This may reflect the comparative relaxation of supply-side constraints to education in the postwar period thanks to the dramatic rollout of schooling opportunities before and after decolonization and independence. But Clemens notes that the evidence of the last half-century suggests that the diffusion of *demand* for educational services still has the key role in explaining outcomes.[32]

Direct evidence of a substantial demand-side influence on enrollment rates is provided by the limited impact of school construction (a "supply-side intervention") on enrollment figures. Deon Filmer of the World Bank looked at enrollment rates in twenty-one developing countries to see if children who lived closer to schools were more likely to attend. At the time, average school enrollment in the rural areas of the study countries was 50 percent. He estimated that if every rural household was right next door to a school, this would increase enrollments by 3 percentage points, to 53 percent.[33]

As with health, cultural factors come to the fore as a reason for keeping children out of school. In Burkina Faso and Pakistan, for example, surveys of poor people revealed a widespread feeling that educating girls made them less attractive marriage prospects. They would be unsatisfied with their marriage options and less skilled at housework. Some interviewees in Burkina Faso went so far as to argue that education was the surest way for a girl to end up a prostitute.[34]

Some countries *have* managed rapid increases in enrollment rates when pent-up demand was satisfied by a new regime that extended schooling opportunities. This was the case in the post-colonial period in a number of countries, or more recently when Uganda introduced free schooling in 1997, for example. And while building more schools appears to have little influence on attendance, demand for education can be stimulated in the same way as demand for health care—we'll see that payments for attendance under conditional cash transfer schemes can have a significant impact on enrollments. Nonetheless, transition speeds are limited by the desire of parents to school their children—a desire that depends in great part on the generational transmission of the idea of the importance of education. This suggests that, as with improvements toward better health, for those countries of the world that are still some way from universal education levels, progress is (almost) certain, but sustainable growth is unlikely to be instantaneous.

THE DIFFUSION OF DEMOCRACY

MIT's Daron Acemoglu and his colleagues think that the global trend toward greater democracy may also be accounted for by the diffusion of ideas. And similar to the s-shaped model of improvement that Michael Clemens finds for school enrollment over time, John Freeman and Duncan Snidal of the University of Minnesota see a common s-shaped curve in the extension of the voting franchise over time in nineteenth-century Europe. The curve suggests that it took approximately sixty years to increase enfranchisement from 10 percent of the adult population to 60 percent. While extensions of the franchise occurred in discrete steps (in Britain, these steps took place under reform bills passed in 1832, 1867, and 1884), the size of the extension was larger if it had been longer since the last extension and if the country was already in the midrange of enfranchisement.[35]

Certainly, since World War II, the *ideas* of democracy and universal rights have proven powerful ones, repeated in numerous documents signed on to by governments throughout the world, as we have seen. Surveys of popular opinion worldwide also point to ubiquitous and considerable majorities in favor of statements such as "democracy may have its problems, but it's better than any other form of government" (ranging from a low of 81 percent in the former Soviet Union to 88 percent in the Middle East and 92 percent in the West).

It is worth noting that while surveys comparing Western and Muslim countries report very similar levels of support for democratic ideals including political toleration, participation, and support for free speech, they suggest markedly different support for gender equality. In this sense, the popular support for universal civil liberties may be somewhat lagging behind that for universal political rights.[36]

Nonetheless, the concepts of both civil and political rights are ubiquitous in both legal and popular opinion worldwide—a circumstance that in no manner prevailed even seventy-five years ago. And while the de jure and the de facto regarding rights can all too often be some considerable distance apart, the power that the *idea* of rights can have is made clear by the snowballing of democratic change across borders. Think, for example, of the shock wave of communist collapse across Eastern Europe, or the link between the Philippines' expression of "people power" with the support of Cardinal Sin and Cardinal Kim's leadership role in mass Korean protests demanding democratic change the following year. Once the transition to democracy is made to look possible by (peaceful) neighboring example, it often spreads.

THE GROWING UNACCEPTABILITY OF VIOLENCE

In 1961, Stanley Milgram of Yale University began a series of experiments to test how far people would be willing to go in causing pain to a fellow human being under the "right" circumstances. Volunteers were apparently divided at random into "teachers" and "learners." The teachers were instructed by a lab-coated researcher to give the learners an electric shock for each wrong answer on a test they administered—although one that would cause "no permanent tissue damage." For each wrong answer, the shock would get stronger at 15 volts at a time. Researchers encouraged wavering teachers to continue the experiment regardless of the complaints of the learner.

At 120 volts, the learners exclaimed they were in real pain. At 150 volts, they begged to end the experiment and be released. By 165 volts, they were screaming to stop. At 300 volts, the learners shouted that they would no longer answer questions. As the voltage increased, they ceased to respond at all, stunned into near-paralysis.

In fact, the learners were actors—the real experimental subjects were the "teachers." And not one teacher in the experiment ceased administering shocks before the 300-volt level. Two-thirds continued administering shocks until they had reached the last switch on their electrocution machine—450 volts.

Teachers would continue despite showing obvious signs of distress themselves—sweating, stuttering, requests to the researcher to allow the experiment to stop. The will to respect
authority was too strong.

But results changed dramatically if "learner" and researcher
swapped roles. Whatever the protestations of the learners regarding the need to complete the experiment, no "teacher" would
continue zapping a man in a white coat if he told them to stop.
And if there were two researchers who argued over continuing
the shocks, "teachers" universally stopped the experiment. Absent clear cues from authority to do the wrong thing, the experimental subjects behaved humanely.

Milgram's study was prompted by the trial of the Nazi war
criminal Adolf Eichmann in an attempt to understand how so
many people could have committed such obscene acts under his
command. At least in part, the answer appears to be that people
respond to authority and social cues even when those cues are
morally repellent. As well as suggesting something about how
widely the responsibility for acts of torture should be allocated,
the Milgram experiment suggests the importance of institutional
settings, and of social norms, to levels of violence and personal
attitudes regarding acceptable behavior toward others.

The good news is that institutional settings and social norms
in most of the world are increasingly set against the acceptance
of violence. For example, fights to the death as a form of entertainment are seen today as a Roman barbarity, and dueling to
the death is also banned worldwide. Modern sports—even "ultimate fighting"—have complex rules designed to reduce the risk
of permanent injury.

Similarly, punishments for crimes have become less violent
over time. The Bible calls for death by stoning for infractions
such as idolatry, blasphemy, homosexuality, adultery, disrespect-

ing one's parents, and picking up stones on the Sabbath. (This
in turn suggests the best time to blaspheme is the weekend.) Medieval sanctions included branding, chopping off of limbs and
tongues, and being burned at the stake, axed at the head, broken
on the wheel, boiled, flayed, sliced up, disemboweled, crucified,
impaled, crushed, stoned (still), hung by the neck, or starved for
a range of different crimes. Today, the death penalty is a punishment limited to a minority of countries for a few crimes, usually without spectacle. We've even begun being nicer to animals.
Rather than burning cats being the sport of kings (Louis XIV of
France), we arrest sportsmen for dogfighting (Michael Vick of
the Atlanta Falcons).[37]

Again, the supposed attractions of violence appear less obvious to the modern mind than to many thinkers of a previous era.
In Europe and America, the glory of war was oft touted before
the bloodletting quagmire of World War I. Tocqueville argued
that war "enlarges the mind of a people and raises their character,"
Zola that "we must eat and be eaten so that the world might live,"
Nietzsche that it was "petty sentiment to expect much (even
anything at all) from mankind if it forgets how to make war,"
Oliver Wendell Holmes that the one thing "true and adorable"
was "the faith . . . which leads a soldier to throw away his life in
obedience to a blindly accepted duty." More recently military
historian John Keegan concluded, "War . . . may well be ceasing
to commend itself to human beings as a desirable or productive,
let alone rational, means of reconciling their discontents."[38]

One factor behind changed attitudes toward violence may be
an increased valuation of life. Emily Oster's study of sexual behavior in sub-Saharan Africa suggests that people with shorter
life expectancies are more likely to undertake risky activities,
and this helps to explain high infection rates in the region. If you
are likely to get bitten by a mosquito and catch cerebral malaria

tomorrow, the risk of unprotected sex today doesn't look as daunting. But if you are given a bed net and a course of chloroquine tablets today, your views regarding the costs and benefits of unprotected sex might change. The same might well apply to acts of violence: If life in general is brutish and short, the additional risk posed by acts of violence is considerably reduced.[39]

A related factor behind lower levels of violence as well as a greater support for democracy and universal social services might be a growing general sense of empathy. Philosopher Peter Singer suggests that a kernel of empathy is bequeathed to us all by evolution. Over time, he argues, the sphere in which we are empathetic has expanded, creating a growing sense of fellow feeling not just with immediate family but also with our clan, tribe, nation, and even the species as a whole. This expanding sense of fellow feeling is reflected, for example, in the willingness of a gainfully employed resident of Baltimore, Maryland, to pay taxes to support the unemployment checks for an ex–auto worker in Detroit, Michigan—or a (however disgruntled) German to pay taxes toward the bailout of the Greek economy. The world, in short, is becoming increasingly cosmopolitan.[40]

Recent debates over climate change suggest this growing cosmopolitanism at work at the global level. Now that a broad consensus over the *science* of climate change encompasses even many on the flat-earth fringes of thought, the argument has moved on to the *economics* of response—would the benefits of early action outweigh the costs. What is interesting about the resulting benefit-cost analyses on both sides of the debate is that they take the world as the community of interest. The justification for (in)action isn't about the costs and benefits of climate change faced by people in New York, or Russia, or the European Union, but the costs and benefits faced by the whole world. In other words, the well-being of a Nigerian child living in Achalla is valued (pretty much) as highly as the well-being of an American child living in Buffalo or a Brazilian in Sao Paolo. The aim of the benefit-cost analysis is to maximize *global* welfare.

Such analyses, by economists such as Sir Nicholas Stern at the London School of Economics or William Nordhaus at Yale, have provided the academic underpinnings for policymakers who prefer radical and urgent action against climate change as well as for those who would take a more tempered approach. But whatever one's view of the relative urgency of tackling climate change as a priority for global policymaking, the policies suggested have been justified on the grounds of a global equality of worth. According to these models, policymakers should value the welfare of all people of the world the same.

This is a considerable—positively incredible—step in terms of our responsibility to people living in other countries compared to what might be expected if policymakers were all "realists," thinking solely of their countries' self-interest. Of course, the need for such a cosmopolitan attitude might also help to explain why coming to a global deal on climate change has proven so complex. Nonetheless, that there is even a significant effort to *attempt* such a deal may be a sign of the growing sense of a global community.[41]

VIRTUOUS CYCLING FOR FREE

Given that elements of quality of life such as education, health, and rights have been expanding and converging worldwide even where income has not, it seems plausible to argue that there might be a self-sustaining relationship—a virtuous cycle—between these trends.

For example, we have seen the considerable evidence that education impacts health outcomes. And health is both an enabler of and a spur to education as well. Michael Kremer and Edward Miguel link a de-worming program to school attendance in Kenya. Provision of pills to students that protect against hookworm, roundworm, whipworm, and schistosomiasis reduces absenteeism by a quarter (although, intriguingly, it does not improve test scores, which might suggest something about the quality of education in Kenya). In Tanzania, studies suggest that children whose mothers take iodized oil capsules when pregnant are less likely to suffer cognitive damage from iodine deficiency. As a result of this intervention alone, these children progress through grades faster—effectively adding about a third of a year of schooling to the child of a treated mother.[42]

The interlinkage between various measures of quality of life that is as strong as or stronger than the relationship with income is widespread. Education may have a small role in promoting preferences for democracy and reducing domestic violence. The presence of a stable democracy is a surer defense against both civil and international war, as well as against mass killings of civilians, than is income growth. Democratic regimes may also see somewhat faster improvements in life expectancy and literacy than autocracies. Inequality has been associated with crime and death rates from political violence, measures of autocracy, and low levels of educational attainment. These interrelationships surely help to explain the similar patterns of global progress across a range of measures of quality of life.[43]

FACILITATING THE SPREAD OF IDEAS: URBANIZATION AND COMMUNICATION

Urbanization may be another factor in the recent convergence of quality of life. Rural-urban migration has been ongoing at similar rates in fast- and slow-growing developing countries alike.

Marianne Fay and Charlotte Opal at the World Bank found that, across countries and time, income growth can account for only 5 percent of the variation in the rate of urbanization. A common global trend across countries over time and initial levels of urbanization between them are far more important explanatory factors—the same situation that, as we have seen, applies to democracy, education, and health.[44]

Urbanization might be linked to quality-of-life improvements because providing infrastructure and social services to urban residents is easier than providing them to rural populations. Both urbanization and infrastructure access allow for the easier transmission of ideas—including ideas about health, the importance of education, and rights. Roads connect people, allowing for easier spread of the technologies of quality of life. And electricity allows access to modern communications. Once again, mirroring the trends we see for urbanization and quality of life, Bill Easterly finds a significant and similar rate of infrastructure rollout across countries over time combined with little evidence of more rapid rollout in fast-growing countries.[45]

The considerably expanded reach of communications infrastructure in particular has played a powerful role in the spread of ideas. The proportion of households worldwide that had a fixed telephone almost certainly surpassed 50 percent in 2003. And even more rapid growth in access has been driven by mobile telephony. The number of mobile subscribers worldwide increased from 11 million in 1990 to 5 billion in 2010. An estimated 86 percent of the world's population, including a considerable majority of rural populations, already lived somewhere with mobile phone reception in 2004—and it appears quite likely that total telecommunications access rates are higher than that.[46]

This reflects dramatic rollout of access in countries from the richest to the poorest. In Burkina Faso, for example, there were fewer than 7,000 telephones outside the capital city in 1990, serving a population of 8.3 million people spread across an area of over 100,000 square miles. There was no mobile phone service. In 2002, the mobile footprint (the area of the country where a mobile phone signal is available) covered 5.4 million people outside of the capital—more than 50 percent of the population living outside of Ouagadougou. Thanks largely to the mobile revolution, for any given income per capita in sub-Saharan Africa the number of telephone subscribers per capita has increased by a factor of ten or more between 1980 and 2005.[47]

Television has spread at least as far. There was one television set for every four people on the planet in 2003. A recent survey of households in a rural area of Indonesia showed how rapidly the technology spread after villages gained access to electricity. Within two years of electrification, television ownership was 30 percent. Within seven years of electrification, household ownership rates reached 60 percent—this in an area where average incomes were around $2 a day. Compare this to refrigerators, which were owned by fewer than 5 percent of surveyed electrified households. Where there is still no electricity network, people hook televisions up to batteries; indeed, in a number of developing countries, household television ownership rates are higher than official household electrification rates.[48]

And household poverty appears to be no barrier to watching *lots* of television once the set has been purchased. The two-dollar-a-day households with televisions in the Indonesian survey were watching, on average, four to five hours per day—about the same levels reached in the United States. In other developing countries such as India, the average viewer is watching somewhat less—but still, fifteen hours of television a week. This is a lot of time to soak up whatever attitudes and social mores are being expressed in the programming.[49]

Hollywood has always suggested that it plays a central role in positively shaping popular attitudes. Tom Hanks sensitively portrayed the humanity of an AIDS sufferer in *Philadelphia*. *Star Trek* showed that everyone was the same under the latex, and broadcast the first interracial kiss on television. *South Park* has dedicated episodes to topics as diverse as the impact of hybrid vehicles and exploration of religious beliefs. And in *Terminator II* Arnold Schwarzenegger demonstrated the importance of not judging people (or robots) purely on the basis of their appearance.

There may, in fact, be something to Hollywood's boast. Robert Jensen and Emily Oster of the National Bureau of Economic Research studied the social impact of cable and satellite television access in rural India. They found that the introduction of cable or satellite services in a village is associated with higher girls' school enrollment rates, declines in fertility, and increased female autonomy. The impact is large: Within two years of introduction, between 45 and 70 percent of the difference between urban and rural areas on these measures disappears. The effect of cable TV access on fertility rates is as large as that achieved by increasing the length of time girls stay in school by five years.[50]

A study of TV rollout in Brazil might help explain these results. Since the 1970s the Rede Globo network has provided a steady diet of locally produced soap operas. The soaps are no closer to being tales of everyday life than is *Desperate Housewives* in the United States—not least because 72 percent of the main female characters on the Globo soaps have no kids and only 7 percent have more than one. (In 1970, the average Brazilian woman, in contrast, gave birth nearly six times.) But the soaps clearly resonate with viewers. As areas covered by the Globo network expanded over the course of the 1970s and '80s, parents began naming their kids after soap opera characters. Women in those areas—especially poor women—also started having fewer babies. Being in an area covered by the Globo network had the same effect on a woman's fertility as two additional years of education. And it wasn't the result of what was shown during commercial breaks—for most of the time, contraceptive advertising was banned, and there was no government population control policy at all. The portrayal of comparatively "realistic" female characters with few children appears to have been an important social cue.[51]

It seems likely that stronger communications have also supported growing empathy and even global cosmopolitanism. It is an old idea that communications are central to building up fellow feeling. Karl Marx and Freidrich Engels suggested that railways were vital in rapidly cementing the union of the working class in the nineteenth century: "[T]hat union, to attain which the burghers of the Middle Ages, with their miserable highways, required centuries, the modern proletarians, thanks to railways, achieve in a few years," they wrote in the *Communist Manifesto*. Perhaps this is why Republicans continue to underfund Amtrak. But the considerable response of global television viewers to images of famine in Ethiopia, or the tsunami in Asia, suggests that TV in particular is a powerful force for shrinking the emotional distance between peoples within and between countries.

Of course, there is the fear that people watching television aren't socializing with others near at hand—recall Robert Putnam's famed phenomenon of "bowling alone," what he saw as a TV-driven decline in sports leagues and community groups. Harvard scholar Ben Olken finds that better television-signal reception in Javanese villages in Indonesia is associated with substantially lower levels of participation in social activities and with lower measures of trust in others. Reception of an extra channel of television is associated with a decline of about 7 percent in the total number of social groups in a village. This could reduce the face-to-face transmission of ideas and knowledge. But on the plus side, despite the impact on his measures of "social capital," Olken doesn't find any negative impact of TV watching on local governance outcomes. Nor does improved television reception appear to affect the level of discussion in village meetings or levels of corruption in a village road project undertaken during his study.[52]

Alongside televisions and the telephone, the world is connected today in numerous ways that it was not in the past. The reach of newspapers and periodicals is greater than ever before; the distance traveled each year by the average human being has never been longer. And this is as true of countries that have remained poor as it is of those that have become rich—again, remember the traffic jams of Kabul. All of this communication has achieved more than just raising global awareness of slow-motion beach running in a swimsuit. (Although that it *has* done—*Baywatch* boasts a billion viewers in 142 countries.) The growth of global communications has also enhanced the spread of a range of lifesaving and life-enhancing ideas.

GROWING GOVERNMENT

The spread of ideas has made provision of health and education services alongside the guarantee of liberties more widely demanded. In particular, it has increased the demand on *governments* to supply (or at least not impinge on) those services and liberties.

In the mid-1800s, the role of governments in providing public health systems or education was distinctly limited. Few places in the world saw anything close to universal primary education, and nowhere saw anything even resembling universal health care (not that it would have done much good at the time). And calls for a considerable expansion of government service provision (or a universal franchise, or gender equity) were rare indeed.

One hundred years later, the great majority of countries had signed on to the UN Declaration of Human Rights. This document suggested that governments should guarantee not only civil and political liberties but also health care, social security, and free education among a long list of other quality-of-life demands. Many countries have moved some way toward meeting these obligations, including a number of countries that are fairly poor even by nineteenth-century standards. Again, compare the ambitions and extent of social service delivery in areas including education, health, and justice in Britain in the early 1800s to those in Vietnam today. The state is expected to do—and manages to do—far more than states at similar income levels in the past. Spreading the knowledge that governments *could* provide such services and that governments said they *would* provide such services may have helped foster demand that governments *should* provide those services.

This brings us to a final, and very important, factor that rich and poor countries alike have seen develop over the past century—large governments. In 1788, government revenues as a percentage of GDP in the United Kingdom were around 12 percent—almost certainly one of the highest rates in the world. Today, government revenues are closer to 45 percent of GDP in the UK, and this number is hardly out of the ordinary. In the recent past, poor countries have averaged larger governments as a percentage of GDP than have rich countries. The world has witnessed ubiquitous growth and convergence in the size of government, then. A lot of the revenue that these governments raise is wasted, but some is spent on providing access to education, public health services, government information, running elections, and (even) protecting rights. This in turn suggests that big government may be a powerful force behind the growth in global quality of life.[53]

THE TRANSITION TO A HIGH QUALITY OF LIFE

Stagnant and fast-growing countries alike are seeing progress toward improved health, education, and liberties, but rich countries are still relatively healthy and well educated, and poor countries still lag behind. What can account for these seemingly contradictory findings?

We have seen in Chapter 3 that precolonial and colonial history might have played a considerable role in determining current income levels. There is also evidence that health and education outcomes as well as institutional environments dating back to the start of the colonial period are strongly linked to current levels of quality of life across countries. Seventy percent of the variation across countries in male life expectancy can be predicted using data on a country's ethnic fragmentation—patterns of linguistic diversity entwined with precolonial and colonial history—and mortality rates among early colonists in those countries in the nineteenth century and before. Regarding education, Raghuram Rajan, former chief economist of the International Monetary Fund, suggests that variation in the percentage of European settlers in the population in 1900 and gross primary enrollments in 1900 are still related to education levels in 2000. And on the topic of country stability, Simeon Djankov and Marta Reynol-Querol find that settler mortality and population density in 1500 are strongly predictive of the likelihood that a country would descend into civil war in the late twentieth century.[54]

Some countries began the race to improved quality of life at a lower starting point and a later time, then—and they remain laggards in the race to this day. But every indication is that they are catching up. Health, education, security, and rights are similar to income per capita in that technology matters. They are different from income in that the technologies and ideas involved have spread globally, and different again in that the demand side and diffusion of ideas may be larger barriers to improved performance than the supply side. Far more than income, quality of life appears to follow a pattern of exogenous growth.

Yet an "exogenous theory of quality of life" should not be taken to suggest no role for policy reform to improve outcomes. A growing role for governments around the world in service provision may be one factor accounting for a common worldwide rate of change in quality-of-life measures. Furthermore, as we shall see, a number of approaches appear to be successful in increasing the development of new technologies, the diffusion of these technologies, and the spread of ideas and demand.

The role for policy reform at the national and global levels thus remains considerable—both to develop new solutions and to speed the rollout of old solutions to long-standing development problems. This policy agenda is the subject of the next two chapters.

EIGHT

POLICIES FOR QUALITY OF LIFE

....

A little under one-sixth of India's population is made up of Dalits—officially known as a "scheduled caste" and traditionally known as untouchables. In the Hindu caste system, these were the people who performed unclean tasks—butchering, leatherwork, removing feces. Because Hindus thought that the religious pollution attached to these tasks was contagious, Dalits were banned from temples and schools.

India's independence constitution, which went into effect in 1950, banned discrimination on the basis of caste. Since then, a number of laws and policies have been introduced to improve the Dalits' situation, and six decades later they are enjoying some of the progress in quality of life that the country of India as a whole has witnessed. Their children are more likely to live a long life than were their parents, they are more likely to be in school, and they are less likely to be condemned to a few outcast professions.

But Dalits still face a far higher risk of violence and discrimination, they experience higher infant and child mortality, fewer are in school, and after school they earn less than those from other castes with similar levels of education. While in school they are frequently made to sit apart from their classmates, and many health workers refuse to visit their homes. Dalits make up one-fifth of the rural population but two-fifths of the rural poor. As many as 1 million still work as manual scavengers, some in bonded labor, picking up their masters' shit from dry latrines with their bare hands or a piece of tin to carry to the nearest dump.[1]

To say that global development has made progress over the past fifty years is not to suggest that there isn't considerable, unconscionable underdevelopment in many parts of the world. If anything, the progress the world has made only increases the sense of how unconscionable remaining underdevelopment truly is. We've shown that we can make progress, so why can't we make more? This chapter discusses some of the roles for national governments in promoting more rapid, broad-based development.

And to repeat again, money matters to such broad-based development. At very low levels of income it is undeniable that every marginal dollar carries benefits in terms of nutrition, health services, education, access to infrastructure, and a range of elements of quality of life. Furthermore, global income equality, as much as greater income equality within countries, is arguably a good in its own right. Given that, policies to promote economic growth—the classic problem, which we tackled at length in Chapter 2—should be an important focus of governments, to the extent we know what such policies are.

Nonetheless, growth policies are only one element in the agenda for broad-based development. The grail of economic growth should not be used to justify sacrifice of the well-being, freedoms, or lives of a country's citizens. The Soviet Union, particularly in its moments of most rapid economic growth, offered a quality of life degraded by war, starvation, and mass murder. Income generation is supposed to be a means to an end, and the Soviet Union distinctly failed to deliver that end.

In countries poor and rich alike, policymaking should be not merely or indeed primarily about the creation of financial wealth but instead about the maintenance and improvement of the broader quality of life of a country's citizens. And it is not a case of utopianism to argue that such improvements in quality of life can be sustained even absent economic growth; indeed, we've seen that most of the significant improvements in quality of life in regions such as sub-Saharan Africa *have* been sustained absent almost any economic growth.

Related to this broader agenda for development is a distinction between two different sets of technologies of development. Process technologies—institutions—are central to increasing GDP per capita. They are increasingly important to the goals of improved health, better education outcomes, security, and environmental sustainability. But the second set of technologies—ideas and inventions—have played the central role in improving health, education, and security in developing countries to date. Ideas and inventions have also ensured that increasing populations can enjoy quality of life without falling into a Malthusian trap. There remains a considerable role for them to play going forward. This suggests that a balanced focus on broad-based development would demand considerable attention to fostering the creation and diffusion of inventions and ideas.

This chapter outlines some rules for policies focused on the goal of economic growth in poor countries. What little we know does suggest some policy pointers, but what we have learned about the broader determinants of quality of life also suggests an important principle. Income growth should not come at the cost of other elements of quality of life. And while we understand that

dramatic improvements in quality of life cannot be achieved overnight, we do have some evidence of approaches based around
stimulating demand for services that may speed progress. Finally,
with the quality of service delivery increasingly important to
quality-of-life outcomes, there are some approaches that may
improve that quality.

POLICY AND ECONOMIC GROWTH

Policies that countries like North Korea and Zimbabwe follow
are economically ruinous. Confiscating the productive assets of
the country and placing them in the hands of political cronies
intent only on stripping whatever can be immediately sold not
only places both countries continually on the brink of famine
but also makes for an unlikely growth strategy.

But evidence from global studies of economic growth suggests that the kind of extreme policies that North Korea and Zimbabwe follow are the *only* ones to significantly and consistently
impact long-term growth rates. The considerable effort to find
a policy grail of growth based on cross-country experiences has
failed. One-size models don't fit the evidence. For example, Nikita
Khrushchev's boasts that the Soviet Union would bury, wave
bye-bye to, and/or be invited in to run the US economy look
ridiculous in retrospect. Nonetheless, Eastern Europe's economic
performance during the Cold War was respectable—better than
Latin America's, South Asia's, or Africa's. And a strong performance unpredicted by macroeconomic gurus has fueled huge
wealth creation in parts of Asia.[2]

We know that countries that grew rapidly followed a mélange
of market-conforming and market-distorting policies. We know
that countries that didn't grow rapidly followed much the same
pattern. East Asian countries that grew rapidly over the last

thirty years had activist industrial policies, for example—and yet so did a number of African and Latin American countries that recorded fairly dismal growth rates. But it wasn't clear beforehand that what would work in East Asia would fail in Africa. And it isn't clear today that an activist industrial policy would have any more success south of the Sahara than it did twenty years ago.

Again, the finding that institutions matter for long-term economic growth does not translate into a simple set of reform prescriptions. The impact of institutional change is highly context-dependent—the current mix of institutions along with a range of other factors can considerably alter the results of reform. Take the results of trying to formalize rural land ownership in Africa, a staple of the institutional reform agenda since at least the 1930s. Surveys suggest that the evidence of any impact of formal titling on perceived land rights of farmers, credit use, or land yields in the region is often weak. In part, this is because indigenous land systems frequently have greater legitimacy and remain considerably operational even after "formal" titling has been introduced.[3]

Given that sure knowledge regarding growth-inducing reforms is lacking, and given that income is a means to an end of better quality of life, the first rule for economic policymaking should be "Do no harm." Policymakers should avoid policies that call for considerable sacrifice—of resources used to ensure health or learning outcomes, or of freedoms or livelihoods—in the name of more rapid GDP per capita expansion.

A second rule for economic policymaking may be to do good by supporting quality-of-life improvements. Improvements in health or education or rights do not immediately and straightforwardly translate into economic growth—otherwise, increases in income per capita would be as widespread as increases in quality of life. That said, at least some evidence indicates that healthier, more educated societies that better protect rights see stronger economic performance over the long term.

Take the example of health. Interviews with poor people worldwide suggest that more than anything else, they dread serious illness within the family as something that can push a household into inescapable poverty, according to Deepa Narayan of the World Bank. So anything that can reduce the extent of accidents and disease not only has significant quality-of-life benefits but also reduces the risk of immiserating illness. Again, reducing child mortality reduces birthrates, in turn fostering a demographic transition toward more adults per child in the population. This has been linked to better economic performance over the medium term.[4]

Similarly, an agenda focused on rights may help long-term growth performance. The importance of institutions does not translate into a straightforward policy reform agenda, and it may not be clear in a particular case that more or less government is a growth-promoting answer. But reforms that help strengthen the power of civic organizations—greater transparency, improved power of oversight—may have a role in improving the quality of government services, as we shall see. This could translate into broad-based development that includes more rapid economic growth.

There are perhaps some grounds for long-term optimism regarding growth rates worldwide given some evidence of a relationship between growth, on the one hand, and, on the other, education, health, political rights, and so on, all of which are expanding worldwide. But even if policies focused on the broader quality of life fail to promote economic growth, if they achieve only more rapid progress toward better health, education, and security, they are still a great success. That's because improvements in health, education, and security are what we *want* from development, while income is just a tool to help achieve them. And we've seen it is often a cheap, plastic, unreliable tool at that.

THE VIRTUOUS CYCLE AND LIMITS TO PROGRESS

In thinking about the broader quality of life, we should revisit claims that we can end poverty in our lifetime. Sustained progress more rapid than we've seen in the past will be difficult. The underlying forces behind technology diffusion at the country level are themselves slow to change, involving culture, behavior adaptation, and development of both formal and informal institutions—and this limits the rate of improvement in quality of life. We may be able to speed progress somewhat, but current performance is already a historical anomaly, and we should not expect too much.

Nonetheless, while evidence suggests that incremental improvement will be the norm in quality-of-life improvements, this incremental improvement is in historical terms *unprecedented* in its speed and global spread. And some countries have done notably better than the incremental average. Furthermore, there is evidence in favor of a positive cycle of improvement between measures of quality of life themselves. Better health increases educational attendance, education provides better access to new health technologies and lifesaving ideas, and so on.

All of this suggests that committed governments and citizens can play a significant role in fostering rapid development at the level of the community, the country, and beyond. To take three examples, this would involve (1) support for the infrastructure and for the institutional structures that allow for the rapid spread of health knowledge and basic preventative measures, (2) demand and supply of quality education, and (3) demand for and provision of the protection of civil rights. And in fostering quality of life, we can build on the considerable existing successes of citizens and governments across the developing world in terms of improving quality-of-life outcomes to date—including in the supposed "development failure" of Africa.

IMPROVING QUALITY OF LIFE THROUGH THE SPREAD OF TECHNOLOGY AND IDEAS

To improve the quality of outcomes, an important role for government is to support the diffusion of technology and ideas. The minimal role for government is to not stand in the way of such technologies. Take the governor of Kano in Northern Nigeria, who delayed the worldwide eradication of polio in 2003–2004 by refusing to allow vaccination in his state on the grounds that it was a plot to make African women infertile. This made him in large part responsible for recent outbreaks around the world. Polio not only reemerged in nine of Nigeria's closest neighbors but also spread as far as Indonesia, which reported 288 cases in 2005 linked to the Kano outbreak.

In some cases, governments will be able to play an important supporting role in spreading access to technologies. Consider mobile telephone access, which has spread incredibly rapidly in the developing world over the last ten years. For the great majority of countries, this has occurred under a model of competitive private provision, which has proven far more ubiquitously successful than private provision in some other infrastructure sectors. But governments have a vital role as regulators—ensuring that mobile networks connect to one another on fair terms for all consumers, for example.

And in some cases—not least vaccination—governments will be prime movers in fostering dissemination if not direct provision of the technologies of quality of life. Certainly, the great majority of vaccine doses worldwide to date have been delivered by public-sector providers.

This does raise the question of the affordability of service provision. But with government delivery of the most basic of services, it isn't size, but what you do with it, that counts. Haiti has a central government that spends around $530 million a year for 9 million people, or a little shy of $60 per head. This is a little less than 1 percent of what New York City spends per capita on city services alone for the 9 million people who live there. Obviously, Haiti could deliver better services with more resources. So growing the economy and expanding the tax base should be an urgent priority (as should international support for that goal). But we have seen that a basic package of health provision can cost as little as $5 per head per year. Even a country as poor as Haiti, with the right priorities, could improve the quality of life of its citizenry through universal access to quality care at a very basic level.

Ensuring sufficient resources to achieve basic quality health care is as much a matter of focusing resources as of finding additional funds. Take Chad, a country of 9 million people, many of whom live in extreme poverty. The Ministry of Health budget amounts to $6.50 per person per year—a meager sum, but sufficient to pay for the basic package of health care if distributed equally. Sadly, health centers, which actually deliver front-line care, account for only 20 percent of the budget. The rest is sucked up by central and regional administrative levels. Nearly all of the funding that does reach the front line goes to staff pay. The amount spent on everything else in the health centers—things like beds, equipment, soap, uniforms, drugs, and vaccines—comes to 6 cents per person each year.[5]

Again, access to free primary education is affordable for the poorest of countries to provide, if resources are allocated with efficiency. And the preservation of political and civil rights is (sadly) usually as much about the state doing less to abuse as it is about the state doing more to protect. There remains an important role for aid programs in support of improved health and education in developing countries—as well as for a range of other activities. Not least, aid may have a role in promoting better targeting of existing resources to promote development outcomes through approaches like payments for service delivery, discussed in Chapter 9. But sustainable provision of basic health and education services does not require ongoing and massive aid flows, even in most low-income countries.

PROMOTING DEMAND FOR QUALITY OF LIFE

Added to these roles as service regulators or providers, governments have an important part to play in fostering demand for such services.

The potential to create demand is well understood by the private sector, which—with great success—spends billions on marketing even the most peripherally valuable products. Take bottled water as an example. There was a time in major cities like London when drinking the tap water exposed you to the fecal contamination of half the metropolis. Today, however, tap water in major Western cities tends to be relatively safe—indeed, safer than bottled water, which often sees far higher levels of bacterial contamination. Tap water is, of course, far cheaper as well (with costs per gallon between 1.0 percent and 0.01 percent that of bottled water). And it is more environmentally friendly—it doesn't need bottles, or bottling plants, or transportation from the plant to the consumer. Blind tests suggest people can't even tell any taste difference from bottled brands. Despite all of this, the bottled stuff sells: Consumers spend more than $7 billion a year on it in the United States alone.[6]

These sales are driven by highly effective marketing. Think of Fiji Water. That would be bottled water from Fiji, a Pacific Island nation about 7,952 miles from New York as the crow flies—or would fly if it could get that far. Fiji Water sells itself as remarkably green, because this distance makes it "Far from pollution. Far from acid rain. Far from industrial waste." The company's Web site suggests, "We are proud to offer a fine artesian water that is good for people and good for the environment."

The company does admit to the fact that shipping the stuff halfway around the world might contribute a bit to global warming, and that the plastic bottles it comes in end up packing landfills. But the company also suggests that with lighter containers and using the Panama Canal rather than trucking the stuff from LA to the Big Apple, Fiji Water's environmental footprint will be reduced. Apparently such braggadocio works. The company has revenues north of $150 million a year selling an image of purity slapped on a bottle of H_2O.

Of course there are far worse, positively insidious, cases of advertising run amok—even others involving water. Infant formula companies in the developing world that encourage mothers to mix powder with untreated tap water in countries where this really is a major danger have been responsible for the deaths of thousands of children. But there is still something perhaps uniquely impressive about the ability to sell the same stuff as comes out of the tap, only from halfway around the world, in an unbiodegradable container, at a thousand-plus times the price—and on top of that sell it on the grounds that it is *for the sake of the environment.* Imagine if that talent could be used for good, to spread ideas and knowledge that improves quality of life.

Governments have a large role in promoting the spread of such ideas and knowledge, either directly or with the support of civil society organizations. That's because development is not just about giving people what they want; it's also about getting them to want what they need. And an important part of that process is to change perceptions of what is (or should be) normal. It should not be normal for children to have diarrhea. It should not be normal for girls to be kept home as their brothers go to school. It should not be normal for teachers to be absent, for clinics to be empty of supplies and staff, and for police to demand bribes. By changing expectations, approaches like communications campaigns, but also payments for attendance and civil society engagement, can create the demand for a better quality of life. If this demand can be matched with effective responses— better sanitation, school staffing, improved governance—then outcomes can dramatically improve.

One example of the role of knowledge promotion is the effort to stamp out open-field defecation in Bangladesh. Fewer than 15 percent of households have access to latrines in rural areas of the country, making open-field defecation (which is exactly what it sounds like—shitting in a field) the usual method. Existing aid-funded mechanisms to subsidize latrine construction appear to have had limited impact. An approach initially piloted with the support of a civil society organization called the Village Education Resource Center involves community-led efforts to build latrines and eliminate open defecation. Facilitators help communities understand that, as a result of open defecation, people are, in effect, eating their own feces; they also provide ideas for design of low-cost latrines where necessary. Communities, without subsidy, construct these latrines and motivate usage. The approach is reported to have stopped open-field defecation in as many as 2,000 Bangladeshi villages with considerable benefits including dramatically reduced diarrhea levels.[7]

Similar social marketing programs have shown strong results over the last thirty years in promoting the use of sugar-salt solutions to treat diarrhea, breast feeding over bottle feeding, and the use of contraceptives. A diarrheal disease control program that focused on social marketing in Egypt in the early 1980s saw the number of targeted mothers who recognized the danger of dehydration rise from 32 percent to 90 percent. In addition, within the first year of the marketing campaign, the number of mothers who used oral rehydration solution correctly increased from 25 to 60 percent. In the Philippines, an immunization project in the early 1990s used mass media to motivate mothers to bring their children to clinics. The percentage of children in targeted areas who completed an entire series of vaccinations before their first birthday increased from under one-third to over one-half within one year of the program launch.[8]

These kinds of programs can be used more widely to build demand for (quality) health and education services and perhaps also to increase civic engagement.

Television can be a particularly important tool in promoting new ideas and approaches. Given that people in rich and poor countries alike spend so many hours watching TV, a few well-designed public service advertisements could have a significant impact. The 2002 global HIV-prevention campaign *Staying Alive*, sponsored by MTV, was broadcast on television stations that reached nearly 800 million homes around the world. Survey results in participant countries suggest that people exposed to the campaign were more likely to talk to others about HIV/AIDS and more likely to understand the importance of using condoms, discussing HIV/AIDS with sexual partners, and getting tested for HIV.[9]

Direct educational programming can also play a huge role. Forty years' worth of academic studies suggest that kids watching Cookie Monster chew through the fifth cookie as counted off by the Count are more likely to grow up reading books by themselves; more likely to score better in English, mathematics, and science in high school; and more likely to value academic performance. And the positive impact of *Sesame Street* has been replicated all over the globe as the show has been copied across continents. In Mexico, viewers of *Plaza Sesamo* saw benefits in literacy and mathematics. In Turkey (*Susam Sokagi*), Portugal (*Rua Sesamo*), and Russia (*Ulitsa Sezam*), the results were similar. The Bengali version, *Sisimpur*, has been associated with improved learning especially among the rural poor—again, replicating a result in the United States. In Israel, the local version is called *Rechov Sumsum*, and it presents messages of mutual respect between Arab and Jewish children. Survey evidence suggests that kids from both backgrounds became more positive about children from the other culture after watching the show.[10]

A related approach involved expanding literacy through same-language subtitling. Starting in 2002, Rangoli, an Indian TV program that broadcasts songs from Bollywood films, subtitled the clips in Hindi—the language in which they are sung. In the same year, a survey of kids about to start primary school was conducted to measure their literacy levels. Five years later, the same kids were tested again. Of those who were illiterate in 2002 who regularly watched TV over the next five years but did *not* watch Rangoli, 24 percent were ranked as functionally literate in 2007. Five years of schooling alone managed to impart basic literacy to only one-quarter of students—which speaks once again to the educational-quality issue in developing countries. The good news is that of those illiterate kids who went to school *and* regularly watched Rangoli, 56 percent became literate over the next five years. Survey evidence does not speak to potential ancillary benefits including audition success rates on *Pop Idol: India*.[11]

Perhaps even more effective is working with the producers and writers of popular programming to embed information in shows. The impact of Rede Globo soap operas in Brazil and of cable programming in rural India—which changed attitudes toward girls' education, domestic violence, and fertility decisions—suggests the potential of such approaches.

Radio is another powerful technology that has long been used for similar purposes. In the UK, the world's longest-running radio soap opera, called *The Archers*, is "an everyday story of country folk." Launched in 1950 with the collaboration of the Ministry of Agriculture, the program was designed to disseminate productivity-enhancing farming techniques during the postwar years of shortage and rationing. The soap now tackles issues such as marketing organic products and European Union farm subsidies in between the more usual fare of affairs and drug abuse. *The Archers* has spawned a number of imitators. The BBC World Service series *Naway Kor, Naway Jwand* (New Home, New Life), broadcast in Afghanistan, is based on the same idea, but with less infotainment on farming subsidies and more on avoiding land mines. Survey evidence suggests that listeners are significantly less likely to be injured or killed by mines than nonlisteners.[12]

Similarly, evaluation studies have found a considerable impact from radio programming designed to increase civics knowledge in Botswana; to improve literacy rates and educational outcomes in the Dominican Republic, Paraguay, Mexico, Mali, and Thailand; to promote breast feeding in Trinidad and Tobago; to promote public health practices in Nicaragua and Swaziland; and to support the rollout of family planning initiatives in South Korea and Sri Lanka.[13]

LIMITS TO TECHNOLOGY AND MARKETING

While the impact of social marketing suggests an important role for communications technologies, falling into the trap of indiscriminate support for the adoption of *any* technology or communicating *every* new idea carries large risks. Consider the latest technology fad, the Internet kiosk—with percentage usage rates in the low single digits of potential customers in rural areas of developing countries. It turns out that illiterate people living on a dollar a day have limited willingness to pay for computer time to open a Facebook account or download music—especially when they have ready access to cheaper and easier-to-use cell phones when it comes to sending messages.[14]

More broadly, just as the importance of institutions to economic outcomes does not imply a simple recipe for reform involving land titling or privatization, neither does the importance of technology for quality of life involve the unthinking promotion of alleged technological fixes to development problems. The long history of inappropriate technologies pushed upon unwilling recipients in developing countries has left tractors rusting on farm fields, Green Revolution seeds rotting in African warehouses, and computers moldering in government offices.

In particular, regarding technologies for which the great majority of the benefit is to the individual user, if we are not seeing at least some use by poor people at market prices, it is likely to be because individuals in developing countries correctly identify limited benefits to that technology. A considerably less likely reason is that they are being slow, stupid, or ignorant (talent is pretty evenly distributed around the world, which is part of what makes underdevelopment such a tragedy). There may be an important role in promoting the use of technologies, but if technologies aren't adopted even after such promotion, it is likely that the problem is with the technology, not the people.

Similarly, not all uses of existing marketing approaches are positive. We've seen that communications strategies in particular can be used for ill as well as for good. The same applies broadly to health knowledge however it is obtained. Regarding antibiotics, for example, it appears that many patients have learned the power of modern drugs without understanding their limits. Combined with underregulated doctors in private practice or public doctors facing little incentive to correctly prescribe, this has led to a rash of antibiotic overprescription. Overmedication in India is particularly widespread because consumers demand pills, and, for doctors, more patients lead to bigger profits. As we saw in Chapter 7, this is also a growing problem in China, where as many as 98 percent of all medicines issued are mis-prescribed.[15]

Circumstances such as these suggest the need for further efforts at education and communication linked to health knowledge, but they also point up that improving both the institutions of health care and its regulation is an important part of sustaining improvements in health outcomes. In addition, they draw attention to the need for (careful, limited) regulation of communications technologies that ensures truth in advertising.

PAYMENTS FOR PROGRESS

Conditional cash transfers appear to be another powerful tool in expanding demand for basic services connected with health and education. Mexico's Programa de Educacion, Salud y Alimentacion (PROGRESA) provides cash to mothers in return for their children attending school and going to health clinics. An early evaluation found that girls' secondary enrollment in program areas increased by 15 percent, and boys' enrollment by 7 percent. The program even increased enrollment rates among families who weren't getting payment. Being in a village where more children were going to school created an increased social pressure to enroll. On the health side, children who were part of the health program for two years were 40 percent less likely to be reported ill and were around one centimeter taller than children not in the program.

A second example of payments for health involved a program in Rajasthan in India that provided a kilogram of lentils to mothers for each child they vaccinated. The program considerably increased rates of immunization. Combined with an outreach program of monthly camps that provided information and inoculation services, the lentil incentive helped to increase vaccination rates from 5 to 37 percent.[16]

A range of other countries have adapted this model of payments for clinic or school attendance. Conditional cash transfers to encourage parents to send their kids to school have met with success in Bangladesh, Colombia, Pakistan, Nicaragua, Kenya, Honduras, Brazil, and Cambodia. In Cambodia, the payments were focused on girls in the lower secondary school system. Selected families were awarded a scholarship of $45 for each of three years during which their girl stayed in the lower secondary system and maintained a passing grade. This scholarship was effective enough to equalize the probability of enrollment and attendance between girls from poor families and those from rich ones. Absent the program, fewer than one-fifth of girls from the poorest tenth of families in a region were enrolled in school, compared to nearly two-thirds for the richest tenth of households. For scholarship-recipient families, enrollment rates for girls were above 80 percent for all income levels—indeed, slightly higher among the poorest families than among the richest.[17]

As a sign of the importance of social cues to decisions regarding health and education, evidence from surveys of poor people worldwide suggests that access to uniforms is another important part of ensuring school attendance. In Armenia and Georgia, for example, parents spoke of children being so embarrassed by their clothing that they refused to go to school. Parents also reported the stigma of poor dress in school during interviews in Bangladesh, India, and Moldova. A series of child sponsorship programs in rural Kenya since 1995 has provided free textbooks and uniforms to students as well as constructing classrooms. Of the three interventions, only the uniforms have proved effective in keeping children in school. While there is no requirement to wear a uniform in Kenyan schools, there is significant social pressure to do so.[18]

The need for ongoing subsidies and payments to encourage behavior change varies between interventions. In Nicaragua, temporary financial incentives to attend clinics increased attendance even after the withdrawal of payments. It may be that the same will be found over time with education subsidies, given the strong role that the level of parental and community education plays in determining choices regarding the education of children.[19]

But the Kenyan school de-worming program discussed in Chapter 7, which initially provided free medication and saw considerable returns in terms of school attendance thanks to improved health, experienced a dramatic decline in usage when even very small charges were introduced. In schools where the treatment remained free, three-quarters of the children were treated, compared to fewer than one-fifth in schools where families were made to pay thirty cents per treatment (one-fifth of the actual price of purchasing and administering the drug). Much of the benefit of de-worming accrues to the community in which the worm-infested individual resides rather than to the infected people themselves. Educated people who were more likely to understand this were even more likely to drop treatment when it was no longer free—suggesting that free treatment would need to continue in order to sustain health and education gains.[20]

In short, policymakers cannot rely on payments for attendance or subsidies as ways of permanently changing behavior if that new behavior isn't in the clear self-interest of recipients. The flip side of this conclusion is that some of the most powerful uses of conditional cash transfers are when they change attitudes. If payments for girls' school attendance make female enrollment the "new normal" in a community, such payments can be phased out over time. This is a model of sustainable change in quality of life fostered by incentives that governments and the development community should strive for whenever possible.

IMPROVING THE SUPPLY OF SERVICES

But it is also worth noting that, while conditional cash transfers may improve attendance, they do not necessarily improve service quality. Take the quality of education: Forty percent of fifteen-year-old Mexican students fail an internationally comparable reading test passed by all but 5 percent of students in the average member-country of the OECD. This leads to a question worthy of consideration: How high are the economic and social returns to financial inducements to stay in school, such as Mexico's PROGRESA program, if they encourage students to attend classes where they will learn so little?[21]

Again, there is a limit to the value of programs to encourage mothers to go to clinics for child health services if the quality of care they receive is little higher than that provided by a traditional healer. A survey of Tanzanian clinics suggests the potential scale of this problem. Doctors routinely display ignorance of the correct diagnostic procedures for illnesses. This is compounded by a lack of effort—exam-free diagnosis based on one question being routine. Surveyors reported one case they witnessed where a woman came in with a sick baby on her back and, after one question asked from behind the desk where he could not even see the child, the doctor prescribed for malaria. One wonders what the standard of treatment would have been had the surveyors not been in the room. In fact, the child had pneumonia and would have died if it had not been for the intervention of the research team.

One way to improve outcomes in the quality of provision is to match payments for attendance with payments for delivery. Supplier payments for the delivery of health services in Haiti had a large impact on expanded immunization coverage and attended child deliveries, for example.[22]

Another way to improve the quality of supply would be to increase demand for quality from consumers and then link that demand to outcomes. For example, Harvard's Michael Kremer, who has been at the forefront of evaluating the effectiveness of education programs around the world, argues that one way to improve the quality of boys' education is to give scholarships to girls who do well in school. This improves the test scores of boys as well because they compete to equal the improved test scores of their female classmates. At one step further removed, parents who know that their opinions will be taken into account are more likely to provide oversight of school performance. In a repeated finding, decentralization of school management down to the individual school level, when combined with the publication of standardized test results, improves quality—because parents are more likely to become involved in the schooling process.[23]

A number of arrangements can strengthen the link between service providers and consumers in terms of accountability and so improve the quality of service delivery. One is the use of citizen report-card systems to interview consumers about the quality of services they receive from government providers in areas like utility provision, health, and education services and policing. The resulting reports are used to stimulate a dialogue between civil society, local government, and service agencies on reform and improvement of services. In Uganda, the introduction of primary health care citizen report cards as part of a randomized trial led to higher utilization of health services and considerably lower under-five mortality, despite no change in government funding.[24]

The Bangalore Citizen Report Card, launched by a civil society organization called the Public Affairs Centre, was also a catalyst in the improvement of local civil services. The report card surveyed citizens on their satisfaction with a range of public services providers covering water, power, municipal services, transport, housing, telephones, banks, hospitals, taxation, and the police. The first survey, in 1994, found an overall satisfaction level at just 9 percent. After each round of the survey, state government and public agencies launched reforms to improve infrastructure and services in the city. There is now greater transparency in the operations of government agencies and better responsiveness to citizens' needs. Overall satisfaction had increased to 34 percent in 1999 and has climbed further since.[25]

The ability and willingness of government to respond to citizen concerns were a part of Bangalore's success that may be absent elsewhere. Other experiments in community oversight have a mixed record because of limited involvement on the part of citizens or responsiveness on the side of government. Nonetheless, in the right environment report cards and citizen oversight can play a role in spurring governments to improve services.[26]

IMPROVING THE PROTECTION OF LIBERTIES

Survey evidence finding widespread support across the world for statements that countries should be democratic and should protect liberties suggests that the idea of rights has near-universal appeal. This is one powerful reason for their recent spread. That said, the *implementation* of liberty and democracy in a country is immensely complex. As with universal education, setting up the universal franchise may be the comparatively easy part. The harder part might be ensuring that the franchise translates into equitable, stable, and responsive government.

In some countries, what remains the primary challenge is removal of the legal and practical impediments to liberties supposedly guaranteed by a country's participation in human rights treaties—limits on freedom of speech, legal discrimination on the basis of gender or caste. In these cases, the organs of government themselves are often some of the biggest abusers. The global surveys of the attitudes of poor people carried out under the *Voices of the Poor* project suggest that the recurrent themes regarding state institutions are "distrust, corruption, humiliation, intimidation, helplessness, hopelessness and often anger." For example, across developing countries, the police consistently rank as one of the most corrupt parts of government, with extortion and bribery the expected norm for interactions.

While police reform is complex, a tool that can be used to reduce the presence of extortion is reduction of the number of de jure regulations and laws on the books that are routinely ignored de facto. Such laws and regulations do not achieve their original objectives, but they do provide a source of leverage for police on the lookout for a bribe. Perhaps one of the most insidious examples is land regulation. A majority of housing in the urban areas of many developing countries is illegal—most commonly because it does not meet building codes or has been built on government land officially zoned for other economic activities. Police and local officials have considerable power over the residents of such housing—they can threaten eviction or destruction of houses if bribes are not forthcoming. Removing the power of police and local officials to enforce such regulation might be a first step toward creating a police force that has a primary role of protecting rather than abusing citizen rights.

Report cards might also play a role in improving the protection of civil and political rights through pressure for reform of the police and courts. More broadly, growing participation by consumers in monitoring the delivery of public services, if matched by improved outcomes, may be one force toward creating a stronger civil society. In turn, this stronger civil society might be better able to play a role in defending civil rights from government abuse.

Existing measures of governance and civil rights outcomes suggest that many measures of different types of freedom are associated with each other. Measures of progress in holding free, fair, and meaningful elections are consistently higher in countries that also score highly on measures of freedom of speech and religion, rights to a fair trial, and so on. Again, subjective measures of government accountability, political instability and violence, the effectiveness of government, the burden of regulations, the rule of law, and corruption aggregated from indicators made by different academics and agencies across countries are very closely related. All of this suggests that improvement in one area of governance may spill over into other areas, so that government efforts to involve citizen oversight of service provision, or loosening restrictions on press freedom, or rooting out corrupt judges might not only be positive developments in their own right but also help to cement broader progress toward civil freedom. This may be another case of the virtuous cycle of improvements in quality of life discussed in Chapter 7.[27]

Regardless, creating a sense of inclusive community, increasing accountability, and establishing institutions strong enough to deter outright abuses of civil rights is a slow process, and one that can involve backward steps. The global history of rights suggests that there is no foolproof method that even the most civic-minded of political leaders can follow to ensure a sustainable democracy. If the global trend is positive, the road toward an "end of history" brought on by global peace and liberty remains rough and long.

BETTER VALUE FOR MONEY

Most developing-country governments could considerably improve the quality of life of their citizenry without a penny of additional revenue or outside aid. All that would be required is an improved focus on delivering vital services efficiently—which is still saying a lot.

With health, ministries should focus far more on public health measures and the spread of cheap lifesaving habits and techniques such as hand washing and breast feeding. In effective hospital and clinic systems, resources flow away from administrators and hospitals in the capital city to front-line service providers in clinics that focus first on basic preventative care, then on cost-effective treatments including oral rehydration and (judicious) use of antibiotics, and only then on more expensive treatments.

With education, for most students even more important than *free* access is *any* access to some minimum level of quality. Supplier payments might be one answer here, linked to the number of students graduated who receive a minimum score on standardized tests or improve their scores by a given amount over time. There is also a role for targeted incentives for attendance in primary education and beyond.

Regarding the protection of civil rights in peacetime, perhaps the greatest role for governments is to do less but do what they do better. Reducing the potential for government officials and in particular the police and army to abuse their positions of power may be one element of this effort. And across the board, government services will extend their reach and increase their quality if there is a place for vibrant civil society oversight.

Chapter 9 discusses some of the roles for the *global* community that might help accelerate the worldwide trend toward progress in quality of life as well as minimize the size and frequency of retrograde steps. These roles involve support to create technologies that can further improve the quality of life at a given income as well as speed the spread of ideas and institutions that underpin health, education, and rights. And again, because the poorest citizens of the world do still need more income as part of a package of changes required to ensure an improved quality of life, the chapter also discusses the role of the international community in promoting income growth.

NINE

THE GLOBAL AGENDA

....

O nchocerciasis is an infection that has blinded over 300,000 people worldwide. Roundworms transmitted through the bite of a black fly spread throughout a host's body, where they usually live for one or two years. When the roundworms die, their decaying bodies cause an immune response strong enough to destroy nearby host tissue, leading to itching, skin diseases, and, where the cornea becomes so scarred that it turns opaque, a condition known as river blindness.

In 1974, the Onchocerciasis Control Program launched in eleven West African countries. Supported by the World Health Organization, the World Bank, the United Nations Development Program, and the Food and Agriculture Organization, the program began by spraying against black fly. After 1988, the partners also began to distribute the drug ivermectin, provided free of charge by Merck, the manufacturer. Ivermectin disabled the adult fly, preventing both itching and reproduction.

In 2002, the program was closed after virtually eliminating disease transmission in ten of the eleven target countries. Sierra Leone, embroiled in a decade-long civil war, was the one exception. The control program had prevented around 600,000 cases of river blindness and had made 25 million hectares of land safe for cultivation.

This success in the battle against river blindness involved cooperation among some of the world's poorest countries, working together with the support of a number of aid agencies in a coordinated response over many years. Like the fight against smallpox, it is one more example of global progress against diseases that affect some of the world's most benighted areas. And like the fight against smallpox, it suggests that aid agencies can have an important role in improving quality of life.

Policymaking in rich countries can play a major part in improving the quality of life in developing countries—not only through promotion of useful trade, migration, and military policies but also through the judicious and directed use of aid. While aid may not be the most effective foreign policy tool to improve the average quality of life in Asia or Africa or Latin America, it may be a more politically realistic tool than some others. And, creatively used—not least in developing and disseminating technology and ideas, as earlier chapters have suggested—it could play a dramatic role in improving outcomes.

WHY BOTHER CARING?

Before discussing the role for global policymaking in the effort to improve quality of life, however, it might be worth asking why people in the United States or France should care about the quality of life of people in Chad or Laos, and why policymakers in rich countries might want to take account of the concerns of people living elsewhere in designing national policies. The usual, and perhaps most practical, argument presented is that selfish interests dictate that we should care. It is nonetheless worth adding a moral argument to the mix, given the clear evidence that luck is the driving force behind who is rich and who is poor in the modern world.

Self-interest is by far the most common reason given by those in rich countries who support greater aid flows, more migration, or other policies of benefit to the developing world. This argument appears to have been particularly powerful in the realm of trade negotiations, perhaps because there is also an appearance of greater equilibrium in negotiations—both sides lower import barriers as part of the deal. But the argument that more development elsewhere will lead to greater global stability, friendlier diplomatic relations, larger markets for donor country exports, and so on has been applied to less obvious cases than trade or immigration policies. Not least, it was central in persuading the US Congress to support the Marshall Plan—a $12 billion program to support reconstruction in Europe after World War II.

There is a lot to such an argument, even regarding aid. People living in a rich, stable, healthy democracy live as well as they do precisely because the great majority of their fellow citizens are healthy and engaged in productive activity. If all of the children in your kid's school have lice, keeping your kid lice-free is remarkably hard. And if all of your neighbors have lost their jobs or are in danger of doing so, it doesn't matter if your online Beanie Baby auction site is grossing millions a year; your house is going to be worth less than if you were surrounded by other financially successful people. That is one reason why average house prices in Detroit in 2009 were around 1 percent of average house prices in Westwood, Los Angeles.

At the national level, we understand that ensuring the great majority of our fellow citizens are healthy and engaged in productive activity requires civil peace, the rule of law, the provision of infrastructure, education, health, and environmental services, and so on. People argue endlessly over the size of government expenditures and transfers involved, and the relative size of the direct or indirect role for government in provision, or European versus Anglo-Saxon models. But these arguments are in fact about pretty small changes in the overall size of government. In the West, government expenditures as a percentage of GDP vary between about 30 and 50 percent—which is to say, government is large in every rich country. And direct expenditure is only one part of the role of government across all of these countries, which share broadly common positions regarding the universals their citizens should enjoy—education, equality before the law, safety and security, and so on.

Imagine if these universals could be achieved worldwide—that there was a global level of civil peace, infrastructure, health, education, and environmental quality that allowed everyone to engage in healthy, sustainable, and productive activity. Surely, the costs of ensuring such a state of affairs would be far lower than the benefits, just as they are at the national level. Furthermore, just as the benefits of security, infrastructure, universal education, and so on at the country level appear to have benefited rich citizens as much as if not more than they have benefited poorer people, the same might well be true of global security, infrastructure, and education. Rich people in rich countries might be the greatest beneficiaries of all. If we could figure out *how* these services could be globally provided, the costs to the global rich would be dwarfed by the benefits.

The good news, once again, is that it does appear possible to extend global access to at least some elements of the good life, including health and education. We know this because such access is at historically unprecedented highs worldwide, in countries rich and poor alike. Indeed, we've seen that some elements of the healthy life have extended to every citizen on the planet, with benefits for all. Smallpox, once a killer of millions each year, now lives on in only a few closely guarded laboratories. The benefits of this eradication program extend around the globe—no child anywhere requires the smallpox vaccine anymore. Only a few years before global eradication the vaccine was still a requirement in the United States, because of the risk of re-infection from another country, even though the last outbreak in America occurred in 1949.

Vaccination efforts in developing countries produced a global return. More broadly, to the considerable extent that aid, trade, migration, and investment have created larger export markets, cheaper imports, a more skilled domestic workforce, higher returns to saving, greater international comity, and fewer threats to domestic security and health, there is a strong case for an international perspective to domestic policy.

Nonetheless, the "selfish" argument for rich-country policies to account for the concerns of the poorest countries is a partial one. Take the argument that fostering global development will lead to greater domestic security. Fifteen out of nineteen hijackers involved in the September 11, 2001, attacks in the United States were from Saudi Arabia, a country with a life expectancy of seventy-two years, adult literacy of close to 80 percent, and an income per capita of more than $13,000. In other words, if low quality of life were the only cause of joining a terrorist cell, many countries other than Saudi Arabia should have proven the larger source of terrorists. As a rule, terror suspects are richer and better educated than the average in the population from which they are drawn—in fact, a disproportionate number of Islamic fundamentalist terrorists are university-trained engineers. A lack of civil liberties rather than health, education, or income is the stronger link between countries or regions that export terror, but even that link is partial.[1] This suggests that preferential trade access or an increase in aid flows to poor countries is likely to be a weak instrument in the anti-terror toolbox, at best.

Given that the selfish argument for caring takes us only so far, we can find recourse in an additional case based on simple morality. The ethical justification for policies that account for the least well-off across borders rests on principles similar to those in arguments for ensuring a minimum standard of living within individual countries.

We have seen that by far the simplest way to become rich is to be born rich in a rich country. Similarly, if you want to be healthy or well educated, you'd be well advised to be born to a healthy, well-educated set of Swedes rather than to two stunted illiterates (however conscientious and loving) from Mali. Hard work and talent do play a role in determining relative wealth or levels of education, as do eating well and exercising in the case of health. But blind luck—the uterus you gestate in—plays the considerably greater part.

Within countries, it appears to be a widely accepted principle that we should attempt to reduce such inequalities born of fortune. State-sponsored programs that guarantee access to some level of health care and education for children—regardless of the presence, wealth, or interest of their parents—are supported across the political spectrum.

The argument for such principles stopping at the border's edge is threadbare. After all, the borders at issue are as immutable to a child as who their parents are. No infant from Achalla in the middle of Nigeria could have had much say in the Berlin Conference of 1884, which settled the borders of the country. Why such a child born on one side of an invisible line created by some long-dead Victorian diplomat should somehow be less our moral responsibility to protect than a child born on the other side of that invisible line is unclear. As we've seen, at least some evidence suggests that such cosmopolitan views are spreading around the world.

The only reason left for arguing against *trying* to help is that we cannot actually help at all—that providing assistance to developing countries is throwing money down a rat-hole. As the case of the triumph over river blindness suggests, this chapter will argue otherwise. At the same time, the moral responsibility to do *something* doesn't necessarily and easily translate into rules about what we should do.

Imagine if we decided to set some global standards that we believed were the minimum morally acceptable level of quality of life. Perhaps this would involve a certain maximum level of child and maternal mortality or risk of death from violence, perhaps a minimum level of education. This would be akin to a set of Millennium Development Goals based around absolute levels rather than change over time. It would be the moral responsibility of all countries to do what they practically could to ensure that this minimum standard was universally met.

Setting such standards and meeting them are two very different things. As with the current Millennium Development Goals, reaching the minimum morally acceptable standard of life within any particular time frame might prove a challenge. For example, an upper limit marks the rate of progress likely in health and education, which is related both to the flow of ideas and to the quality of institutions in developing countries.

And outsiders in particular are limited in what they can do to improve outcomes in developing countries to reach such a standard. This is because both institutions and the channels through which knowledge and ideas flow are country-specific, so that "global expertise" may have limited local applicability and we face considerable uncertainty as to what works.

Furthermore, however much one hopes that judging people's worth or worthiness based on their citizenship is as anachronistic as judging them on their race, sex, or creed, sovereign states are still imbued with considerable legitimacy. That means there is a limit to the role that foreign intervention can or should play in ensuring global minimum standards.

But a level of uncertainty regarding the best approaches to improving global quality of life, the extent of global income distribution implied, the speed with which it can be accomplished, and the exact role for the global community should not cloud the bigger picture. We don't know if a dollar spent on a second flat-screen TV has any impact on the well-being of a child in America. But we do know—at least to some degree—the likely impact of a dollar spent on an insecticide-treated bed net on the health of a child in Kenya. Whatever the uncertainties regarding the most efficient policies and approaches to improve quality of life for the most disadvantaged in the world, they are not so large as to diminish the imperative to act. A number of methods (such as free bed nets) have improved outcomes for some of the most disadvantaged globally. And if these efforts *might* work if more broadly applied, they are surely worth trying.

THE SCOPE OF GLOBAL POLICYMAKING

Some of the most robust tools for wealthy countries to help improve quality of life in developing countries fall outside the usual areas of focus of aid agencies. Not least, migration to the developed world is perhaps potentially the most powerful force of all for improving the quality of life of people in poor countries.

Movement of people from areas of little opportunity to areas of rapid growth has greatly reduced the impact of regional inequality on national inequality across the world. According to Lant Pritchett, whose work we've drawn on time and again, migration is the driving force for overall income convergence within countries. And Pritchett estimates that if rich countries increased their labor forces by only 3 percent through reduced restrictions on migrant labor, this would add $300 billion to the welfare of citizens of poor countries—roughly four times the magnitude of current foreign aid flows. Migrants themselves see considerably improved health and education outcomes, and there are spillover effects in terms of quality-of-life impact in their countries of origin.[2]

Furthermore, from a simple economic perspective, borders that are open to people, like borders that are open to goods, are likely to be good for the countries on the receiving end. At the extreme, it may be that the social dislocation and adjustment costs of a rapid move to fully open borders are high. But most countries are a long way from that risk. Pritchett's 3 percent solution, especially if focused on immigrants from some of the world's poorest countries, would have a dramatic impact on development and should be plausible. In the United States, for example, approximately 10 percent of the population is (already) foreign-born without any apparent disintegration in the social or political fabric of the country. And there is a strong moral case for the freer flow of peoples across borders. Again, why should the villager from Achalla be prevented from free movement by lines drawn up by Europeans 150 years ago?

Turning to a morally more complex area of international relations, we find that armed force has ended periods of mass murder and returned a semblance of peace to Uganda (removing Idi Amin) and Cambodia (the Khmer Rouge). And state collapse related to civil war is one of the few shocks powerful enough to considerably slow progress in quality of life over the medium term, suggesting the importance of stability to broad-based development. This suggests at the very least a role for international peacekeeping. But many exercises in regime change or country stabilization, however well intentioned, have only made situations worse. Military action to curtail humanitarian catastrophe has a place in the toolbox of those countries concerned with improving the lot of the world's most deprived, but it is a tool of last resort.

Other methods carry less risk of increasing the toll of violence on the quality of life in developing countries. Restrictions in the trade of arms and in the production of weapons such as mines can reduce the power of militaries to inflict suffering on civilians. And restricting trade in the goods that provide financing for armed conflict also has a considerable role. The Kimberly Process, designed to prevent the sale of diamonds sourced from areas of civil conflict by recording where they are produced and tracking them through the distribution chain, is one initiative in that direction.

While trade in arms has had a negative impact on the quality of life of the world's citizens, trade in products such as vaccines and antibiotics has had a direct and very positive impact on health in developing countries. Even if the link between levels of trade and rapid economic growth appears fragile, trade in goods has been a central factor in reducing the cost of quality of life around the world. It has also freed countries from the Malthusian trap through food imports. This makes the failure of the recent round of World Trade Organization talks on further trade liberalization an undoubted loss.

International trade negotiations have had some significant negative implications for the quality of life of the world's poorest, nonetheless. They have begun to impinge dramatically on the free flow of knowledge and ideas around the world, by strengthening the intellectual property laws that restrict such flows.

Copyrights and patents are important policy tools to encourage creativity and innovation, which have been central to the development of technologies that have lowered the cost of quality of life. But excessively strong intellectual property protections can have the opposite effect—stifling innovation and restricting the use of new technologies. The ongoing expansion of copyright and patent protections in the rich world is rapidly tilting the scales toward this stifling of innovation. For example, the character Mickey Mouse was granted a copyright extension thanks to recent US law, despite the fact that it is unclear how such an extension could influence creator Walt Disney's incentives to be imaginative—he's been dead forty-plus years, after all.

On top of that, developed countries are putting significant pressure on the developing world to strengthen their own intellectual property protection as part of international and bilateral trade treaties, including those under the umbrella of the World Trade Organization. Average copyright and patent protection periods in developing countries increased from between four and seven years prior to the last round of World Trade Organization agreements to a minimum of twenty years after the agreements were put in place. This has had an estimated cost to developing countries, purely in terms of licensing payments, of $20 billion per year. And US bilateral trade agreements are adding twenty years to copyright terms above World Trade Organization rules, while weakening the rights of countries to override this artificial monopoly in cases of national emergency.[3]

To meet World Trade Organization commitments, the Indian parliament has banned unlicensed production of generic versions of drugs still under patent. The copycat-drugs industry in

India had forced down the annual cost of AIDS treatment from $15,000 per patient to a little more than $200 in less than ten years, but the new rules stifle this competitive pressure. A recent study by Carsten Fink, now the chief economist of the World Intellectual Property Organization, suggests that there will be significant welfare losses to Indian patients as a result of the law.

Stronger intellectual property protection, some argue, will foster economic growth in developing countries, by encouraging the expansion of creative industries—but the evidence for this is thin indeed. And even if this growth effect were to materialize, expanding monopolies of knowledge and ideas are still likely to slow the transfer of cheap technologies to the developing world. Given the greater importance of cheap technology over marginal increases in wealth to improvements in the global quality of life, any such trade-off is unlikely to be worth it.[4]

But does the existence of generic or knockoff drugs decrease the incentives to develop new vaccines and treatments to tackle major diseases in the developing world? Generics undoubtedly reduce the profit margins for the original drugmaker. However, such a concern would be more persuasive if there was evidence that drug companies significantly consider developing-country markets when choosing where to focus their research efforts in the first place. In fact, priorities are set by the considerably more lucrative markets of the developed world. Why consider re-searching a vaccine for a disease that infects people who spend perhaps ten or twenty dollars a year on health care when people in the United States are spending nearly six thousand dollars a year?

That Merck could afford the generosity of giving away the drug that controls river blindness is a sign of its limited impor-tance to the company's bottom line. Merck doesn't, and doubtless couldn't afford to, give away Propecia—the drug they developed to combat male pattern baldness, which is a big seller in the United States. This suggests that patents and copyrights are doing a poor job in focusing research expenditure where there is maximum health impact.

Indeed, American pharmaceutical firms spend two and a half times more on marketing and administration than they do on research and development. Comparing the expenditure for creating supply of new drugs to the expenditure for creating demand for them might suggest something about their apparent value. Writing as a balding male, I can still say that whatever the twisted market created by intellectual property rights suggests, ending river blindness does more for the global quality of life than combating the scourge of the comb-over.[5]

If we want to see greater research and development for diseases that plague the developing world, far better than imposing the bludgeon tool of intellectual property protection would be methods to provide direct incentives for research into particular diseases—an approach discussed later in the chapter.

AID AND QUALITY OF LIFE

Even if aid is not the most important channel though which rich countries affect the quality of life of people living in poor countries, it is a potentially powerful tool. The "aid effectiveness" literature that has focused on links between aid flows and economic growth might give us some pause, however.

The majority opinion of academic studies does appear to be that aid, at least in certain circumstances, might promote growth. This result is, to bastardize Samuel Johnson, like a dog's walking on his hind legs. It is not done well, but you are surprised to find it done at all. One recent literature survey found thirty-four studies suggesting an aid-to-growth link, although the results are statistically weak.[6]

Most aid-effectiveness studies tend to find little or no significant relationship between aid flows and economic growth in general, but many do find such a link if they split results by recipient characteristics (for example, "good policy" recipients, those with "strong institutions," or "non-tropical" recipients), by type of aid (netting aid for social sectors or particular donors), or by timing (Cold War and after). Accordingly, it might be accepted that recent low-interest loans to richer countries currently receiving little aid—and with reasonable macroeconomic policies, strong institutions, and cool climates—are likely to be some of the aid flows most positively associated with growth. If the aid supports projects that are cofinanced by the recipient government and designed to have a short-term payoff, all the better.

As with most statistical analyses of growth, these results are fragile, but they suggest that the average donor's most effective (growth-promoting) aid policy might be to keep all the aid at home and buy itself a new road. A second-best strategy would be to give aid to rich, institutionally strong developing countries that appear to need it least.[7]

How do we explain this less-than-stellar performance? In part, it is not immediately clear why we would expect transfers received from rich countries to foster economic growth in poor countries. After all, it is not the usual justification for income transfers *within* rich countries that they will lead to more rapid long-term income growth among poor households.

Furthermore, as we saw earlier, mounting evidence suggests that many of the institutional factors that do promote stronger economic performance are difficult to change by policy fiat. And there are even reasons why we might expect aid to hurt long-term growth prospects. One such reason echoes once more the welfare debate in rich countries—the potentially debilitating effects of dependency. That's the argument Dambisa Moyo makes in her recent book *Dead Aid*. Aid engenders laziness on the part of African policymakers,[8] she suggests in one of her attacks on the aid industry.

Moyo may overplay the evidence at points, but dependency is a significant issue. For a sample of African countries in a recent study, aid was equal to an average of 14 percent of GNP and 43 percent of government spending. And there is *some* evidence that large aid flows are associated with lower local tax collection and a declining quality of democratic institutions. Grants appear to reduce domestic tax collection particularly in countries plagued by high corruption, where the decline in taxes associated with increased aid flows may be larger than the aid flows themselves.[9]

In addition, the management of a fractured aid program can put a considerable burden on a developing country's limited institutional capacity. The average country receiving aid is host to twenty-six bilateral and multilateral donors, in return for an average aid package of only $13 million per donor per year. Between 2000 and 2002, Tanzania hosted an estimated 1,300 donor-financed projects, 1,000 donor meetings a year, and 2,400 reports due per quarter. That's a lot for any country to handle, let alone one with Tanzania's limited resources.[10]

Aid aimed specifically at improving the strength of institutions—which might counter some of these debilitating effects—is hard to evaluate rigorously. Regardless, there isn't a lot of evidence that it is strongly effective, which should come as no great surprise. We have seen that the "technology" of institutions flows across borders with difficulty, and that institutional reform is likely to be highly context-specific. This may suggest a comparatively limited role for the diffusion of "best practices"

and technical assistance based on the model of international con-
sulting experience—a common aid-funded model.[11]

Where does this leave us? The implication is that aid specifically focused on promoting economic growth is most difficult
to deliver to precisely those countries that need it most. And
this might lead us to revisit some of the main recommendations
regarding policies for growth from Chapter 8. As pointed out
there, a key principle should be "Do no harm"—aid to promote
growth is not worth sacrifices in health or education or rights.
And one potentially positive channel for aid may be "Do good"—
focus on health, education, and rights—because such changes
are beneficial in and of themselves in the short term and may
improve economic outcomes over the long term. More important, the fact that quality-of-life improvements can be sustained
absent GDP growth suggests that aid does not have to increase
GDP per capita in order to be declared a success.

AID FOR OTHER GOALS

Of course, this only raises the question of whether aid can improve other outcomes more reliably than it appears able to sustain economic growth. Analysis at the global level is patchy, but
what there is echoes the findings of the literature on aid and
growth. Some of the few cross-country studies of aid effectiveness in terms of nonincome outcomes suggest that aid flows in
general have a weak relationship with improved health or education, but the only solid signs of a positive impact are where
there are strong institutions in place.[12]

That said, we need not rely on the jerry-rigged lemon of cross-
country growth modeling in order to examine the relationship
between aid-funded programs and health or education outcomes

in particular. In previous chapters, we have seen that a range of conditional cash transfer programs, payments for service delivery, vaccination and de-worming programs, and communications campaigns aimed at improving quality of life have had an impact that has been rigorously evaluated. And a great number of these interventions were aid-funded.[13]

It is true that these interventions have been proven at the micro level—involving outcomes in a particular school or health district. Under other circumstances, they may not have worked so well. And it may be that rolling them out nationwide or in other countries would tax the limited capacities of local health or education ministries. But anyone who thinks we can't use considerably more aid effectively despite such capacity constraints is suffering from a lack of imagination.

First, we could reduce the capacity requirements of aid flowing through ministries perhaps even while increasing the development impact of such aid. One potential model to achieve greater impact with lower capacity costs is through a national equivalent of the payment-for-service-delivery model that we have seen working within countries at the provider level. Nancy Birdsall of the Center for Global Development has championed such a model. It would involve paying governments a fixed sum for evidence of progress against pre-agreed, easily measured targets. Examples might include a payment for each additional student who completed primary or secondary education taking a set of standard tests, or each additional child vaccinated against a series of major diseases. Donors would not interfere in the "how" of service provision with extended missions and armies of consultants, nor demand particular procurement practices or financial audits. They would pay purely on evidence of results based on independent surveys.[14]

Second, even if there may be declining returns to more aid using the traditional model of working with national governments, there are still considerable opportunities to work with particular communities or provinces within countries—perhaps again using a system that demands comparatively little of local bureaucracy such as payments for progress.

GLOBAL PROJECTS

Third, given the importance of technology and ideas to global outcomes, there is also a role for donors to support the research and dissemination of innovations friendly to broad-based development. Aid might support new vaccine development, such as the partially effective malaria vaccine currently under trial in Africa developed by Glaxo SmithKline with the support of the Gates Foundation. Or aid might support the creation of more robust vaccines—vaccines that do not require refrigeration, for example, or that are simple for nonexperts to administer. Aid could support the creation of new solutions that are simple to apply even absent strong institutions—perhaps a onetime treatment for tuberculosis to replace the current treatment, which involves a series of clinic visits over months. Beyond vaccination, the research agenda might include the development of new prophylactic tools against malaria or diarrhea, or the development of cheap but robust housing materials, or approaches that allow teachers with limited training to perform better in the classroom.

A comparatively traditional approach to technology-focused development assistance could be modeled on the Consultative Group on International Agricultural Research, an effort founded in the aftermath of India's Green Revolution that seeks to replicate the dramatically increased crop yields achieved in the subcontinent throughout the developing world. The Consultative

Group supports fifteen centers dedicated to research into sustainable increases in agricultural output. It has played an important role in ensuring that the world as a whole has escaped the Malthusian trap. Perhaps a similar model might be adopted for research into appropriate technologies and approaches (including high-quality evaluation) that could significantly reduce child mortality, for example. The research center model may also be appropriate for developing communications approaches that show a robust, reliable, and replicable impact on the speed of knowledge transfer at the community level—perhaps using community radio, advertising, or other methods of social marketing.

A second approach might be to use financial incentives to encourage private research. One model promoted by Britain's Department for International Development is the advanced purchase commitment.[15] The department, along with a number of other donors, has committed resources to a fund that will be used for the purchase of a vaccine to protect against pneumococcal diseases (including pneumonia and meningitis). Specifically, the $1.5 billion commitment made by these donors is guaranteed to be used to purchase a vaccine that meets minimum effectiveness criteria under a given price ceiling, providing an incentive to pharmaceutical companies to undertake vaccine development.

A similar approach might work for an advance purchase of vaccines for AIDS, malaria, and tuberculosis. The advance purchase model might also be used to purchase new seed varieties with particular attributes designed to increase yields in Africa, for example, or to buy off-grid renewable power sources that could work reliably and cheaply in developing country settings.

Another approach is that of using prizes to provide an incentive to research. Prizes played a role in the development of accurate timepieces required to measure longitude at sea; they also provided the incentive for Charles Lindbergh to fly across the

Atlantic nonstop. More recently the model has been exploited by the X-Prize Foundation, which offered $10 million to the first company to launch a reusable three-passenger vehicle one hundred kilometers into space twice within two weeks. The foundation is already working to develop a prize based around the creation of a cheap and effective diagnostic tool for tuberculosis and is considering a range of prizes in education.

Given the centrality of technology and ideas to development progress, and the range of approaches that have shown some promise at the local and global levels in extending knowledge and innovation, it may be that there is a role for a new or existing multilateral development organization to expand support in this area. Such a global innovation bank would foster research into new technologies and approaches to tackle development challenges as well as methods to speed the adoption of such technologies. It could use a combination of traditional research funding methods, advance purchase commitments, and prizes to provide this support.

Of course, a global innovation bank would face a considerable risk of funding white-elephant technologies. The history of aid projects is littered with efforts that foist inappropriate technologies on unwilling recipients, with negligible or even negative impacts, as we have seen—rural Internet kiosks, Soviet tractors employed en masse in Ethiopia in the 1980s, "revolutionary" seed varieties that fail in poor soils or intermittent rains, solar stoves that cook during the day when people want hot food at night.

That technological fixes can be as risky or counterproductive as the policy silver bullets discussed in Chapter 3 suggests that any global innovation bank should have as a core mission rigorous and independent selection and evaluation procedures. Project selection should be based on strong evidence of potential demand and potential impact—not on an assumption that "we

v best" and that demand will emerge when recipients learn
understand what we already know. And, where possible, eval-
ation should rely on the same kind of techniques required for
testing new drugs—randomized approaches where participation
is decided by lottery. Failing that, evaluation should at the very
least involve rigorous survey and analysis to determine what
works, what the required preconditions are, and how sustainable
are the resulting approaches. If a global innovation bank were
able to focus its efforts on the development and diffusion of technologies and ideas with real utility to poor people in developing
countries, it could provide a considerable return to aid resources.

AIDING THE FIGHT AGAINST
NEO-MALTHUSIAN THREATS

Supporting efforts to sustain the global commons is an additional, self-evident, and important role for financial transfers
from rich to poor countries. Rich countries want developing
countries to follow a low-carbon path to development because
if the latter use the same technologies that the United States and
Europe adopted as *they* got richer, sea levels will rise by meters
at a time. Rich countries want poor countries to join in efforts
to reduce overfishing because the former have already been
doing it for four hundred years and we are running out of fish.

At the same time, it is worth making two caveats. First, traditional models of aid to promote sustainability might face many
of the same difficulties as models of aid to promote economic
growth, because sustainability involves the protection of common goods (like the atmosphere), which no one person owns.
In turn, this requires complex institutional structures including
regulation and regulatory bodies, which are difficult for aid to
support. Second, as with aid to promote growth, a fundamental

principle should be "Do no harm" to quality-of-life prospe
otherwise, aid justified largely on the grounds of avoiding rr
world mistakes will end up costing poor people in the developir.
world. Neo-Malthusian issues matter because they are a global
threat to broad-based sustainable development—and so responses to neo-Malthusian threats should be judged on their relative efficacy in *promoting* broad-based sustainable development.

That said, climate change is a significant threat to the prospects
for sustained and improved quality of life in developing countries. And unsustainable fishing or forestry practices are a poor
choice for developing countries for purely selfish reasons, regardless of any global impact they might have. Furthermore, there are
a number of potential projects for aid that would have a significant positive impact on the quality of life in developing countries
while simultaneously reducing threats to sustainability.

For example, efforts to extend access to electricity powered
by renewable resources can have considerable benefits for the
environment, health, and broader quality of life in developing
countries. The use of traditional fuels by around one-half of the
world's households puts significant stress on local environmental
commons. Demand for wood for cooking, for example, can be
a significant force for local deforestation. Such fuels also lead to
significant local and global pollution. At the local level, nitrogen
oxides, dioxins, polycyclic aromatic hydrocarbons, other volatile
organic compounds, and fine particulate matter all contribute
to a heavy burden of acute respiratory infections, which in turn
are responsible for perhaps 2 million deaths annually. At the same
time, cooking with wood or dung on a hearth is a very inefficient
system, creating far higher emissions of carbon dioxide and
methane per degree of heating achieved than do modern stoves.
And if these traditional methods can be replaced with electric

heating and cooking systems powered by alternative energy sources such as solar or wind, both the local and global pollution costs can be reduced to near zero. There is a role for direct support to countries to roll out sustainable energy networks, then, but also for a significant level of indirect support in areas such as technology development at the global level to reduce the cost and complexity of on- or off-grid renewable power provision.[16]

AIDING THE RIGHT AREAS OF DEVELOPMENT

We have seen that aid to promote stronger institutions has a somewhat mixed record, perhaps in part because "institutional technologies" do not flow easily across borders. At the same time, we have seen that invented technologies and ideas appear to be central both to sustaining the global escape from the Malthusian trap and to improving quality of life worldwide. The more straightforward path for aid, then, is to focus primarily on developing and diffusing technologies and ideas rather than on institutions. We should not abandon the effort to strengthen institutions, as they are both central to vital economic growth in the poorest countries and increasingly important to broader quality-of-life outcomes. But we should be cautious with regard to global best practices and aware of the likely limits to the speed and extent of change that can be fostered by aid.

A related area that this chapter has left undiscussed so far is the role of donor programs in promoting the observance of civil rights. It is likely that the best things that donor countries can do to extend democracy are, first, to lead by example; second, to avoid sustaining regimes that practice widespread civil rights abuse by supporting them with aid or military assistance; and, third, to make democratic reform a condition of full integration (involving trade, finance, *and* migration)—a model practiced by the European Union with potential candidate countries.

Nonetheless, considerable resources have been ploughed into more direct interventions such as supporting elections, training judges and journalists, and funding civil society organizations dedicated to protecting rights. Such activities are hard to evaluate rigorously. Absent direct evidence, it appears likely that aid for building the institutions of democracy would have as patchy a record as other aid for institution building. And thus it might be wise to lower expectations of outcomes regarding such aid. Still, to return to the argument that opened this chapter, even money spent on aid with potentially low returns is, from most moral standpoints, probably better spent as aid than as the marginal purchase of a family bearing the average tax burden in the United States or Europe.[17]

The good news overall is that the hope for aid doesn't rest on the back of very old cases like the Marshall Plan or marginally-better-than-inconclusive cross-country studies. Instead, the hope for aid rests on a growing raft of success stories covering interventions in health, education, and beyond and stretching from the local to the global. The evidence is clear that there is a range of ways to reallocate existing aid resources and to use new resources to good effect in terms of global quality of life. Even if the current global aid architecture is imperfectly designed to support sustainable increases in quality of life, it is still possible to design aid policies that would considerably improve global outcomes.

And again, the success of development—the fact that things are getting better—makes the moral case for greater aid flows compelling. The only convincing reason why a child born through no choice of his own in a country with borders created by capricious whim is less our responsibility than one born somewhere else is if we believe that the very presence of a country border makes us unable to help. But if aid *can* work to improve quality of life in other countries, that one convincing reason does not apply. The success of development is by far the best reason to support continued and expanded aid flows.

TEN

CONCLUSION

Realistic Optimism

....

The four horsemen of the apocalypse are on the retreat. A century of development has seen considerable tragedy—world war, genocide, mass starvation—but, globally, rates of absolute income poverty have fallen dramatically even as populations have grown. Every region has escaped the Malthusian trap. And in every region more children are being educated, people are living longer, and liberties have expanded. Even the concept of stagnation can only fairly be applied if we limit ourselves pretty much to one indicator (GDP per capita) and one region (Africa). From a long-term perspective, the idea of crisis ill fits the evidence of how the world is getting better.

Not least, the last century saw an unprecedented change in the nature of human health. Infant mortality declined from ubiquity to a rarity worldwide and adults lived longer across the globe. This development occurred everywhere. It did not require rapid economic growth to sustain it, suggesting instead that the spread of cheap technologies and approaches were the key—technologies such as immunizations, antibiotics, boiling water, washing hands, and using latrines. And the spread of these technologies has become even more rapid over time. We saw that it took 180 years between the introduction of a smallpox vaccine and the disease's global eradication. The world as a whole saw only 1,349 cases of polio in all of 2010—this only fifty-four years after Jonas Salk developed the first polio vaccine.

A reason for additional hope is that the countries that are furthest ahead in terms of providing quality of life are those countries that began providing public goods the earliest—public goods including basic educational services and a system of rights. Now, even many countries previously colonized under the most oppressive regimes are striving to provide such services to citizens. This suggests that the future may see these countries (continue to) progress toward greater quality of life. Humanity has never been in better shape—and despite growing challenges of global sustainability, the future should be even brighter.

Nor have we ever been closer to the collective and peaceable solution of global challenges from war to environmental degradation, and poverty. While some argue that original sin, or native inhumanity and irrationality, condemns the species to violence and dispute, the evidence is increasingly against them. The number of international wars has dramatically declined over the recent past. The number of international treaties is inexorably on the rise, covering issues ranging from trade and ozone depletion to human rights. Perhaps more important, adherence to such treaties is on the rise as well.

Of course, this book is hardly the first attempt to combat dystopian worldviews, but such views are remarkably resilient. And more optimistic interpretations of recent world history appear largely limited to the right wing—not least *The Improving State of the World* by Indur Goklany, or *In Defense of Global Cap-*

italism by Johan Norberg—both of these authors have worked at the right-leaning Cato Institute.

That the Right should have a seeming monopoly on optimism is strange. Life, after all, has been getting better in a lot of countries that are unlikely to be short-listed for the Ayn Rand Award for Doctrinaire Adherence to Laissez-Faire. Indeed, life has been getting better pretty much everywhere at pretty much the same rate—under (semi)socialist and (comparatively) free market regimes alike. Worldwide, a century of unprecedented global improvement in quality of life was also one of unprecedented growth in the size of government.

And optimism is vital to the case for aid—hardly an expenditure darling to the Right. Reporting widespread success is no call for complacency. Quite the reverse. That there has been widespread success suggests how much we can achieve. The strongest argument against a moral imperative to act to improve things for the worst-off is that we are powerless to make things better. Global progress gives the lie to that hopelessness and strengthens the case for action—dramatic, expensive, large-scale, publicly funded action.

Calls for aid based on (realistic) hope rather than (exaggerated) fear would make a nice change. The Pearson Report back in 1968 used the clarion of crisis to call for a response from rich countries of much-increased aid flows, equal to 0.7 percent of their GDP. Forty years later, those calling for increased aid are using the same language. Surely it is time to retire it. It does not help to generate the resources for bed nets, or vaccines, or potable water if we continually cry "crisis." Suggesting that the governments and nongovernmental organizations that have long struggled to deliver the services required for improved outcomes have failed so miserably over the last thirty years that we remain in crisis surely suggests that more resources to these same actors would only be a waste. That if there is still a crisis, development actors have only themselves to blame. That more money to the same cause would be money down a rat-hole.

In fact, governments and civil society organizations have been central to improved outcomes across the developing world. These all too often corrupt and usually inefficient organizations have nonetheless played a role in a widespread, unprecedented revolution in quality of life over the last fifty years. Governments and civil society organizations have been key to expanding educational opportunities, to improving access to infrastructure, to providing basic health care. This success, rather than continued failure leading to crisis, is surely the reason that developing-country governments and their development partners deserve continuing, growing support that would have us reach or surpass the 0.7 percent aid target.

And, regarding Africa in particular, the idea that the region would have been better off had it lacked access to the technological cornucopia of the last two hundred years just doesn't stack up against the evidence. The region has seen better health, higher education, and improvements in the broader quality of life that have been the result, not least, of this very technology. Without it, there would have been a lot fewer Africans living a life considerably more nasty, brutish, and short.

This is not to say all technology has been an unalloyed good— look at the AK-47–wielding child soldier of the Lord's Resistance Army in Uganda and that much is clear. And technology has created urgent problems for the planet—climate change, the risk of outright planetary annihilation through global thermonuclear war. Nonetheless, it has also brought immense benefits for people rich and poor in countries North and South. That technology has made quality of life ever cheaper means that very high incomes—and their associated environmental costs—are less and less a necessary element of the good life.

Africa's not-inconsiderable progress also gives the lie to notions that the region is suited for nothing but recolonization. Around the world and across the ideological spectrum there is a great deal of confidence that we "know" the cause of what ails Africa (even though Right and Left disagree on what it is we know). Given that we do not even seem to be clear about what the ailment is, this confidence is likely to be misplaced.

In terms of policy within and toward Africa, this record suggests three things. First, we should be humble—we are unclear as to the record and the reasons for Africa's successes and failures (this applies as much to thinkers of the Left as to those of the Right). Second, our view of African states should not be one of contempt for their failure. Only if we use a narrow, partial view of what "success" meant for the people of the continent can "failure" be the verdict without caveat. Given this, the West's willingness to partner with African governments and African people should be based not on an assumption of unfettered superiority of approach but, instead, on one that recognizes the significant accomplishments of independent Africa to date. Finally, we should be realistic in the goals that we set. If Africa's growth record has not been atypically poor over the last forty years, it might not be that much higher over the next forty. Again, building demand for health and education and improved quality of government takes time, so progress, while historically rapid, will remain incremental.

Another caution of humility involves the conclusions of this book. We have seen that most "recent" growth theories are just retreads from Keynes or Smith. Similarly, that there's more to life than money is hardly a novel line—Samuel Preston made this point using cross-country data more than forty years ago, and the creators of the GDP measure were themselves concerned with the issue. They in turn could have quoted Adam Smith's *Theory of Moral Sentiments,* completed in 1759, to make the same argument, and Smith could have quoted the Ancient Greek tragedy of King Midas to illustrate his case. It is an old and obvious idea that we should have a broad view of what constitutes the good life.

But when we accept this idea, we uncover a view of progress increasingly at odds with a view centered on income alone. This old idea is increasingly current, then, and gives valuable insights into a continued evolution in the global quality of life. Never before has it been more important to understand that there is more to life than money—both to understand the past success of development and to ensure that the world continues getting better.

ACKNOWLEDGMENTS

I would like to thank coauthors on papers and articles that form the basis for some of the material presented in this book: Michael Clemens, Ursula Casabonne, Todd Moss, and David Williams. Thanks to the journals that published some of those papers, including the *Journal of International Development*, the *Asian Economic Policy Review*, the *European Journal of Development Research*, *World Development*, the *Journal of Development Studies*, *Kyklos*, the *Journal of Environment and Development*, *Foreign Policy*, and the *Harvard International Review*. In particular, thanks to those who edited and reviewed the papers (many anonymously) for what were frequently multiple rounds of trenchant and helpful criticism.

Tim Sullivan at Basic Books much improved the draft with a keen eye for the redundant. Christine Arden's copyedits further improved the manuscript. For comments on parts or all of the draft, thanks to Michael Benedikt, Paul Currion, John Daly, Richard Easterlin, Joshua Gallo, Indur Goklany, Carol Graham, Cornlio Hopmann, Anthony Kenny, Nancy Kenny, Pamela Kenny, Andy McLennan, Stephen Mc-Groarty, Todd Moss, Al Rio, Gaute Solheim, Michael Warlters, and "The Disagreeables" book club.

In addition, I put a draft of the book online for comments. Many thanks to Felix Salmon for an initial link and some generous comments. Thanks also to Matt Yglesias, Tyler Cowen, and Brad DeLong for blogging the draft. Beyond attracting interest from publishers (not least Basic Books), the process elicited some very valuable suggestions and corrections. Errors are mine, as are the views expressed.

NOTES

CHAPTER 1, ABANDONING HOPE

1. Kaplan, 1996, p. 27; Collier, 2007, p. 3; Ferguson, 2005.

2. Moyo, 2009; Clark, 2008, p. 3.

3. Figures are from Penn World tables: http://pwt.econ.upenn .edu/.

4. Pritchett, 1997, p. 1.

5. A search of Google Scholar conducted on August 8, 2007, entering the phrase "East Asian Miracle" returned 6,530 hits. Quote from Felipe, 1999, p. 36.

6. Regarding the two articles, Sachs argues that, while point estimates and some implications changed from one paper to the next with the addition of geographic variables, the important benefits of good policy remain significant—the articles are different, but not contradictory (see Kenny and Williams, 2001; Sachs, 1996; and Sachs, 1997).

7. See Kenny, 2005a.

8. Easterlin and Sawangfa, 2009.

9. See Easterly, 2008, and Kenny, 2005b.

10. This paper count is also from Google Scholar.

11. Twenty-two out of thirty-five of Jesus Christ's reported miracles are about healing or raising people from the dead, while others are about curing the sick. Many of the rest involve expelling evil spirits— surely a related subject. Even Saint Donatus, whose first miracle involved getting a deceased woman to tell her husband where she had put the rent money, quickly graduated to banishing demons and bringing people back from the dead.

12. Available online at www.who.int/immunization/newsroom/ Global_Immunization_Data.pdf, accessed April 26, 2009.

CHAPTER 2, THE BAD NEWS

1. Gies and Gies, 1991.

2. Income estimates are based on Maddison (2001) and on an income share of the bottom 40 percent of approximately one-half the national average income. Note that "poorest" in the first sentence is meant in terms of income, while the ownership data are based on the poorest 40 percent in terms of asset ownership. Filmer and Pritchett (1998), from whom the asset ownership data are drawn, argue that the two are closely linked.

3. Gross national product (GNP) is a better measure, because it adds net earnings of a country's citizens abroad, but (a) it is harder to calculate and (b) in most cases the numbers are fairly similar (in the United States they differ by 0.5 percent).

4. DeLong, 1992.

5. Cooper, 2005.

6. Milanovic, 2008.

7. Maddison, 2001.

8. Bourguignon and Morrisson (2002).

9. Sala-i-Martin, 2002; World Bank, 2004; Bourguignon and Morrisson, 2002; United Nations, 2007.

10. This global distribution discussion is based on Milanovic, 2002. The data are as provided by Milanovic except that Yemen and the bottom 10 percent of urban Argentina and New Zealand are dropped from the sample (reported annual incomes were given as $3.30 and $195, respectively). Data on income deciles are from Dikhanov, 2005.

11. World Bank, 2008c.

12. Kenny and Kenny, 2006.

13. Bowles and Gintis, 2002.

14. It is equivalent to an income of around $60 million a year. Assuming that income comes from capital earning a little under a real 5 percent return, this gives a net worth of around $1.3 billion, enough to get onto the 2008 Forbes 400.

CHAPTER 3, THE WORSE NEWS

1. Quoted in Escobar, 1994, p. 25.

2. The quotes are from Sachs, 2005, p. 11. See also UN Development Project, 2005.

3. Easterly, 2006, p. 6.

4. Devarajan, Easterly, and Pack, 2003.

5. Putnam, with Leonardi and Nanetti, 1993; Fay, 1993; Grenato, Inglehart, and Leblang, 1996; Seabright, 1997.

6. Easterly et al., 1993.

7. Schaffer, 2004; Miguel and Roland, 2006.

8. Data from Maddison, 2001.

9. Aisbett, 2005, p. 32.

10. Aisbett, 2005.

11. The search was for papers that included the words "cross-country," "economic," "growth," and "regression."

12. Easterly, 1999b.

13. Levine and Renelt, 1992.

14. Pritchett, 1996.

15. World Bank, 2008c.

16. Rodríguez, 2006.

17. Keynes, 1933, p. 285.

18. Perkins and Perkins, 1999.

19. Holmes, 2008.

20. Acemoglu, Johnson, and Robinson, 2001.

21. Engerman and Sokoloff, 2005.

22. Nunn, 2008.

23. Comin, Easterly, and Gong, 2006.

24. Spolare and Wacziarg, 2006.

25. Gartner, 2005.

26. Barro and McCleary, 2003.

27. Diamond, 1997.

28. Kenny, 1999.

29. Heilbroner, 1963.

30. The course was for the Teachers' College at Columbia University, and the instructor was Edward Resiner.

31. Acemoglu, 2008, p. 3.

32. Ferguson, 2005.

CHAPTER 4, THE GOOD NEWS

1. Sen, 1999.
2. Clark, 2007.
3. Pereira, 2006.
4. Bar and Leukhina, 2006.
5. Data from Maddison, 2001.
6. Kenny, 2010.
7. Ruttan, 2002; Goklany, 2002; Goklany, 2009.
8. Kenny, 2010.
9. Conley, McCord, and Sachs, 2007; Osili and Long, 2007.
10. Diamond, 2005.
11. Ponting, 2007.
12. Note, however, that estimates since then have ranged from 1 billion to 1,000 billion people, with even the last few years seeing variation from 3 billion to 40 billion. So it looks like we don't know much more than we did 330 years ago. See Clark, Crutzen, and Schellnhuber, 2005.
13. Kenny, 2007.
14. Kristoff, 2008.

CHAPTER 5, THE BETTER NEWS

1. Narayan with Patel, Schafft, Rademacher, and Koch-Schulte, 2000.
2. Clemens, Kenny, and Moss, 2007.
3. Maddison, 2001.
4. Morrisson and Murtin, 2005.
5. Calculated from Abouharb and Kimball, 2007.
6. Kenny, 2005a.
7. Data from World Bank, 2007.
8. Calculated from data in World Bank, 2007.
9. Kenny, 2005a, partially updated with figures from World Bank, 2009.
10. Kenny, 2005a.
11. Morrisson and Murtin, 2005; Kenny, 2005a.
12. Benavot and Riddle, 1988; World Bank, 2007. Note, however, that the World Bank figures and the Benavot and Riddle figures do

not measure enrollment in the same way—one source uses net and the other gross enrollments.

13. Based on data from Morrisson and Murtin, 2005; this and the following are unweighted statistics.

14. Tooley, 2005.

15. Keith, 2002.

16. This calculation on average global Polity scores is based on a simplifying assumption, in that the average available Polity scores are not weighted (Kenny, 2008a).

17. Pinker, 2002; Eisner, 2003.

18. Heinemann and Verner, 2006; Kenny and Kenny, 2006; Easterly, Gatti, and Kurlat, 2006.

19. Pinker, 2007.

20. Where "major" is defined as causing 1,000 battle deaths for colonial or international wars, or 1,000 civilian or military deaths related to battle for civil wars; data from Mueller, 2007. See also Milanovic, 2005.

21. Kenny, 2005a; Heinemann and Verner, 2006.

22. Thanks to John Daly for this story.

23. Goklany, 2002.

24. Filmer, Hasan, and Pritchett, 2006.

25. Clemens, 2004.

26. Tooley, 2005.

CHAPTER 6, THE GREAT NEWS

1. Quoted in Hirschman, 1977, pp. 106–108.

2. Belton and Whittaker, 2007.

3. Income figures are from Banerjee and Duflo, 2006—although the authors note that even those living on a dollar a day spend as much as 8 percent of their income on tobacco and alcohol. Food price figures are from World Bank, 2008b. See also Leipziger, 2008.

4. Pritchett and Summers, 1996; World Bank, 2005; World Bank, 2008a; Deaton, 2006.

5. UN and World Bank, 2007.

6. Ravallion, 1997.

7. Kenny, 2008b.

8. Banerjee and Duflo, 2006.
9. Kenny and Kenny, 2006.
10. Preston, 1975.
11. Kenny, 2008b.
12. Kenny, 2005a.
13. Lipset, 1959; Kenny, 2008b.
14. Cutler, Deaton, and Lleras-Muney, 2006.
15. Kenny, 2008e; Easterly, 1999a; Kenny, 2008c.
16. Acemoglu and Robinson, 2006.
17. Kenny, 2008a.
18. Mueller, 2007; Kenny and Kenny, 2006; Djankov and Reynal-Querol, 2008.
19. Heinemann and Verner, 2006; Fajnzylber, Lederman, and Loayaza, 1998; Human Security Centre, 2005.
20. Easterly, 1999a.
21. See Kenny and Kenny, 2006, for a review.
22. Kenny, 2008b.
23. Lindeboom, Portrait, and van den Berg, 2003; Moradi, 2006. See also Diener and Diener, 1995.
24. Pritchett, 1997.
25. See Frech and Miller, 1996, for a partial review.
26. Preston, 1975.
27. This was argued by Ingram, 1994.
28. Kenny, 2008b.
29. Weil, 2005.
30. Collier, 2007.

CHAPTER 7, DRIVERS OF THE BETTER LIFE
1. Diamond, 1993.
2. Dennett and Connell, 1988; Pinker, 2002.
3. Kenny and Casabonne, 2008.
4. Rees et al., 2008.
5. Kenny and Casabonne, 2008.
6. Clemens, 2004.
7. Acemoglu and Robinson, 2006; Easterly, 1999a.
8. Goklany, 2002.
9. Ruttan, 2002.

10. Soares, 2007.

11. Komlos, 1994.

12. Riley, 2001.

13. Reller et al., 2003.

14. Boone and Zhan, 2006.

15. Birchenall, 2007.

16. The analysis is based on data from Bourguignon and Morrisson, 2002.

17. Behbehani, 1983. Cost estimate for the Big Dig from the *Christian Science Monitor*, December 12, 2003: "$14.6Bn Dollars Later, the Big Dig Wraps Up." The five movies are *Pirates of the Caribbean: Dead Man's Chest, Pirates of the Caribbean: At World's End, Superman Returns, Spiderman 3*, and *King Kong*. This is assuming that the $312 million total is expressed in 1970 US dollars (which is not clarified in Behbehani, 1983); see www.wikipedia.org for the costs of the films. It is worth noting that the movie review Web site www.rottentomatoes .com gave these movies an average rating of 62 percent, which is a barely passing grade. The World Health Organization's performance should surely be rated considerably higher.

18. Comin, Easterly, and Gong, 2006; Soares, 2007; Kenny and Casabonne, 2008.

19. Jones et al., 2003; Boone and Johnson, 2008.

20. World Bank, 2006; Loevinsohn and Harding, 2005.

21. Kenny, 2008c; Younger, 2001; Filmer, Hammer, and Pritchett, 2000.

22. See Ranis and Stewart, 2001, on the link between health-sector outputs and outcomes.

23. Liu, Hsiao, and Eggleston, 1999; Eggleston et al., 2007.

24. Boone and Johnson, 2008; data on regional child mortality from Claeson et al., 2000.

25. Jenkins and Scott, 2007; Boone and Johnson, 2008.

26. Boone and Zhan, 2006.

27. Soares, 2007; see also Kenny, 2008b, for more references.

28. Hazra et al., 2006; Jayachandran and Kuziemko, 2009.

29. Beith, Eichler, and Wiel, 2007; Regalia and Castro, 2007.

30. Sadique and Asadullah, 2006; Luby et al., 2004.

31. Kenny, 2008b.

32. Clemens, 2004.

33. Filmer, 2004.

34. Narayan et al., 2000.

35. Acemoglu and Robinson, 2006; Freeman and Snidal, 1982.

36. Diamond, 2007.

37. Pinker, 2009.

38. Quoted in Mueller, 2007.

39. Oster, 2005.

40. Singer, 2002.

41. See Kenny, 2007, for a review.

42. Kremer and Miguel, 2004; Field, Robles, and Torero, 2008.

43. Thorbecke and Charumilind, 2002; Heinemann and Verner, 2006; Chong and Gradstein, 2009; Vollmer and Ziegler, 2009.

44. Fay and Opal, 2000.

45. Easterly, 1999a.

46. Kenny and Keremane, 2007.

47. Based on data from World Bank, 2007.

48. Madon, 2003; McNeil and Letschert, 2005.

49. Rajivan, 1999.

50. Jensen and Oster, 2007.

51. La Ferrara, Chong, and Duryea, 2008.

52. Olken, 2007.

53. Ferguson, 2001; Arnett, 2001.

54. Kenny, 2008b; Djankov and Reynal-Querol, 2008; Rajan, 2006.

CHAPTER 8, POLICIES FOR QUALITY OF LIFE

1. See Kijima, 2006, and Kabeer, 2006.

2. Easterly, 2005.

3. Easterly, 2008.

4. Narayan et al., 2000; Bloom, Canning, and Sevilla, 2001.

5. Garrett, 2007.

6. Lalumandier and Ayers, 2000.

7. Pasteur, 2005; Kar, 2003.

8. Ling et al., 1992.

9. Geary et al., 2005.

10. Fisch, 2005; Cole et al., 2003.

11. Kothari, Bandyopadhyay, and Bhattacharjee, 2008.

12. Andersson, Whitaker, and Swaminathen, 1998.

13. See Eltzroth and Kenny, 2003.
14. See Kenny, 2006, for a review.
15. Das, Hammer, and Leonard, 2008.
16. Holla and Kremer, 2008.
17. Filmer and Schady, 2008.
18. Narayan et al., 2000; Holla and Kremer, 2008.
19. Regalia and Castro, 2007.
20. Kremer and Miguel, 2007.
21. Filmer, Hasan, and Pritchett, 2006.
22. Das, Hammer, and Leonard, 2008.
23. Kremer, Miguel, and Thornton, 2004; Di Gropello, 2004.
24. Bjorkman, Reinikka, and Svensson, 2006.
25. Ravindra, 2004.
26. Banerjee et al., 2006.
27. De Mesquita et al., 2005; Kaufmann, Kraay, and Mastruzzi, 2003.

CHAPTER 9, THE GLOBAL AGENDA
1. Krueger and Maleckova, 2003; Abadie, 2006.
2. Pritchett, 2006.
3. Fink and Reichenmiller, 2005.
4. Fink, 2005.
5. Angell and Relman, 2002.
6. McGillivray, 2005; Doucouliagos and Paldam, 2005.
7. See Kenny, 2008d.
8. Moyo, 2009.
9. Brautigam and Knack, 2004; Rajan and Subramanian, 2005; Gupta et al., 2003.
10. Acharya, Fuzzo de Lima, and Moore, 2006; Knack and Rahman, 2004.
11. Coviello and Islam, 2006.
12. Burnside and Dollar, 1998; McGillivray, 2005.
13. Levine, 2007
14. Birdsall and Savedoff, 2010
15. Levine, Barder, and Kremer, 2005.
16. Donohoe and Garner, 2008.
17. Coviello and Islam, 2006.

BIBLIOGRAPHY

Abadie, A. 2006. "Poverty, Political Freedom and the Roots of Terrorism." *American Economic Review* 96, no. 2.

Abouharb, M., and A. Kimball. 2007. "A New Dataset on Infant Mortality 1816–2002." *Journal of Peace Research* 44, no. 6.

Acemoglu, D. 2008. "Interactions Between Governance and Growth: What World Bank Economists Need to Know." In World Bank, ed., *Governance, Growth and Development Decision Making*. Washington, DC: World Bank.

Accmoglu, D., S. Johnson, and J. Robinson. 2001. "The Colonial Origins of Comparative Development: An Empirical Investigation." *American Economic Review* 91, no. 5.

Acemoglu, D., and J. Robinson. 2006. *The Economic Origins of Dictatorship and Democracy*. Cambridge: Cambridge University Press.

Acharya, A., A. Fuzzo de Lima, and M. Moore. 2006. "Proliferation and Fragmentation: Transactions Costs and the Value of Aid." *Journal of Development Studies* 42, no. 1.

Aisbett, E. 2005. "Why Are the Critics So Convinced That Globalization Is Bad for the Poor?" NBER Working Paper 11066.

Andersson, N., C. Whitaker, and A. Swaminathen. 1998. *Afghanistan: The 1997 National Mine Awareness Evaluation*. Kabul: UNOCHA.

Angell, W., and A. Relman. 2002. "Patents, Profits and American Medicine: Conflicts of Interests in the Testing and Marketing of New Drugs." *Daedalus* 2, pp. 211–234.

Arnett, A. 2001. "Social Fractionalization, Political Instability, and the Size of Government." *IMF Staff Papers* 48, no. 3.

Banerjee, A., and E. Duflo. 2006. "The Economic Lives of the Poor." MIT Department of Economics Working Paper 06–29.

Banerjee, A., et al. 2006. "Can Information Campaigns Spark Local Participation and Improve Outcomes? A Study of Primary Education in Uttar Pradesh, India." World Bank Policy Research Working Paper 3967.

Bar, M., and O. Leukhina. 2006. "Demographic Transition and Industrial Revolution: A Coincidence?" Society for Economic Dynamics 2006 Meeting Paper No. 383.

Barro, R., and R. McCleary. 2003. "Religion and Economic Growth." NBER Working Paper No. 9682.

Behbehani, A. 1983. "The Smallpox Story: Life and Death of an Old Disease." *Microbiological Reviews* 47, no. 4.

Beith, A., R. Eichler, and D. Wiel. 2007. "Performance-Based Incentives for Health: A Way to Improve Tuberculosis Detection and Treatment Completion?" Center for Global Development Working Paper 122.

Belton, S., and A. Whittaker. 2007. "Kathy Pan, Sticks and Pummelling: Techniques Used to Induce Abortion by Burmese Women on the Thai Border." *Social Science and Medicine* 65, pp. 1512–1523.

Benavot, A., and P. Riddle. 1988. "The Expansion of Primary Education, 1870–1940: Trends and Issues." *Sociology of Education* 61, no. 3, pp. 191–210.

Birchenall, J. 2007. "Economic Development and the Escape from High Mortality." *World Development* 35, no. 4.

Birdsall, N., and W. Savedoff. 2010. *Cash on Delivery: A New Approach to Foreign Aid with an Application to Primary Schooling.* Washington, DC: Center for Global Development.

Bjorkman, M., R. Reinikka, and J. Svensson. 2006. "Local Accountability." Stockholm University Institute for International Economic Studies Seminar Paper 749.

Bloom, D., D. Canning, and J. Sevilla. 2001. "Economic Growth and the Demographic Transition." NBER Working Paper 8685.

Boone, P., and S. Johnson. 2008. "Breaking Out of the Pocket: Do Health Interventions Work? Which and in What Sense." In W. Easterly, ed., *What Works in Development? Thinking Big and Thinking Small.* Washington, DC: Brookings.

Boone, P., and Z. Zhan. 2006. "Lowering Child Mortality in Poor Countries: The Power of Knowledgeable Parents." LSE CEP Discussion Paper 0751.

Bourguignon, F., and C. Morrisson. 2002. "Inequality Among World Citizens: 1820–1992." *American Economic Review* 92, no. 4.

Bowles, S., and H. Gintis. 2002. "The Inheritance of Inequality." *Journal of Economic Perspectives* 16, no. 3, pp. 3–30.

Brautigam, D., and S. Knack. 2004. "Foreign Aid, Institutions, and Governance in Sub-Saharan Africa." *Economic Development and Cultural Change* 52.

Burnside, C., and D. Dollar. 1998. "Aid, the Incentive Regime, and Poverty Reduction." World Bank Policy Research Working Paper 1937.

Chong, A., and M. Gradstein. 2009. "Education and Democratic Preferences." IADB Working Paper 684.

Claeson, M., E. Bos, T. Mawji, and I. Pathmanathan. 2000. "Reducing Child Mortality in India in the New Millennium." *Bulletin of the World Health Organization* 78, no. 10.

Clark, G. 2007. "The Long March of History: Farm Wages, Population, and Economic Growth, England 1209–1896." *Economic History Review* 60, no. 1.

———. 2008. *A Farewell to Alms: A Brief Economic History of the World*. Princeton, NJ: Princeton University Press.

Clark, W., P. Crutzen, and H. Schellnhuber. 2005. "Science for Global Sustainability: Toward a New Paradigm." Harvard CID Working Paper 120.

Clemens, M. 2004. "The Long Walk to School: International Education Goals in Historical Perspective." Center for Global Development Working Paper 37.

Clemens, M., C. Kenny, and T. Moss. 2007. "The Trouble with the MDGs: Confronting Expectations of Aid and Development Success." *World Development* 35, no. 5.

Cole, C., et al. 2003. "The Educational Impact of Rechov Sumsum/Shara'a Simsim." *International Journal of Behavioural Development* 27, pp. 409–422.

Collier, P. 2007. *The Bottom Billion: Why the Poorest Countries Are Failing and What Can Be Done About It*. Oxford: Oxford University Press.

Comin, D., W. Easterly, and E. Gong. 2006. "Was the Wealth of Nations Determined in 1000 BC?" NBER Working Paper 12657.

Conley, D., G. McCord, and J. Sachs. 2007. "Africa's Lagging Demographic Transition: Evidence from Exogenous Impacts of Malaria Ecology and Agricultural Technology." NBER Working Paper 12892.

Cooper, R. 2005. "A Half-Century of Development." CID Harvard Working Paper 118.

Coviello, D., and R. Islam. 2006. "Does Aid Help Improve Economic Institutions?" World Bank Policy Research Working Paper 3990.

Cutler, D., A. Deaton, and A. Lleras-Muney. 2006. "The Determinants of Mortality." NBER Working Paper 11963.

Das, J., J. Hammer, and K. Leonard. 2008. "The Quality of Medical Advice in Low-Income Countries." World Bank Policy Research Working Paper 4501.

Deaton, A. 2006. "Global Patterns of Income and Health: Facts, Interpretations, and Policies." NBER Working Paper 12735.

DeLong, B. 1992. "Growth in the World Economy ca. 1870–1990." Mimeo, Harvard University.

De Mesquita, B., F. Cherif, G. Downs, and A. Smith. 2005. "Thinking Inside the Box: A Closer Look at Democracy and Human Rights." *International Studies Quarterly* 49, no. 3.

Dennett, G., and J. Connell. 1988. "Acculturation and Health in the Highlands of Papua New Guinea." *Current Anthropology* 29, no. 2.

Devarajan, S., W. R. Easterly, and H. Pack. 2003. "Low Investment Is Not the Constraint on African Development." *Economic Development and Cultural Change* 51, no. 3.

Diamond, J. 1993. *The Third Chimpanzee: The Evolution and Future of the Human Animal.* New York: Harper.

———. 1997. *Guns, Germs and Steel: The Fate of Human Societies.* New York: W. W. Norton.

———. 2005. *Collapse: How Societies Choose to Fail or Succeed.* New York: Penguin.

Diamond, L. 2007. *The Spirit of Democracy: The Struggle to Build Free Societies Throughout the World.* New York: Times Books.

Diener E., and C. Diener. 1995. "The Wealth of Nations Revisited: Income and Quality of Life." *Social Indicators Research* 36.

Di Gropello, E. 2004. "Education Decentralization and Accountability Relationships in Latin America." World Bank Policy Research Working Paper No. 3453.

Dikhanov, Y. 2005. "Trends in Global Income Distribution,
1970–2000, and Scenarios for 2015." Human Development Report Office Occasional Paper.

Djankov, S., and M. Reynal-Querol. 2008. "Poverty and Civil War:
Revisiting the Evidence." CEPR Working Paper DP6980.

Donohoe, M., and E. Garner. 2008. "Health Effects of Indoor Air
Pollution from Biomass Cooking Stoves." *Medscape Public
Health & Prevention: Public Health Perspective.* Accessed online
at http://www.medscape.com/viewarticle/572069 on November
3, 2008.

Doucouliagos, H., and M. Paldam. 2005. "Aid Effectiveness on
Growth: A Meta-Study." University of Aarhus Department of
Economics Working Paper 2005–15/6.

Easterlin, R., and O. Sawangfa. 2009. "Happiness and Economic
Growth: Does the Cross-Section Predict Time Trends? Evidence
from Developing Countries." Institute for the Study of Labor
Discussion Papers 4000.

Easterly, W. 1999a. "Life During Growth." *Journal of Economic
Growth* 4.

———. 1999b. "The Ghost of Financing Gap: Testing the Growth
Model Used in the International Financial Institutions." *Journal
of Development Economics* 60, no. 2.

———. 2005. "National Policies and Economic Growth: A Reap-
praisal." In P. Aghion and S. Durlauf, eds., *Handbook of Economic
Growth.* Amsterdam: Elsevier.

———. 2006. *The White Man's Burden: The Wacky Ambition of the
West to Transform the Rest.* New York: Penguin.

———. 2008. "Can the West Save Africa?" *Journal of Economic Literature* 47, no. 2.

Easterly, W., R. Gatti, and S. Kurlat. 2006. "Development, Democracy and Mass Killings." CEPR Discussion Paper No. 5715.

Easterly, W., M. Kremer, L. Pritchett, and L. Summers. 1993. "Good
Policy or Good Luck? Country Growth Performance and Temporary Shocks." *Journal of Monetary Economics* 32, no. 3.

Eggleston, K., L. Ling, M. Qingyue, M. Lindelow, and A. Wagstaff. 2007. "Health Service Delivery in China: A Literature Review." *Health Economics* 17.

Eisner, M. 2003. "Long-Term Historical Trends in Violent Crime." *Crime and Justice* 30.

Eltzroth, C., and C. Kenny. 2003. "Broadcast and Development: A Role for the World Bank?" World Bank Working Paper 11.

Engerman, S., and K. Sokoloff. 2005. "Colonialism, Inequality and Long-Run Paths of Development." NBER Working Paper 11057.

Escobar, A. 1994. *Encountering Development.* Princeton, NJ: Princeton University Press.

Fajnzylber, P., D. Lederman, and N. Loayaza. 1998. *Determinants of Crime Rates in Latin America and the World.* Washington, DC: World Bank.

Fay, M. 1993. "Illegal Activities and Income Distribution: A Model with Envy." Mimeo, Columbia University.

Fay, M., and C. Opal. 2000. "Urbanization Without Growth: A Not So Uncommon Phenomenon." World Bank Policy Research Working Paper 2412.

Felipe, J. 1999. "Total Factor Productivity in East Asia: A Critical Survey." *The Journal of Development Studies* 35, no. 4.

Ferguson, N. 2001. *The Cash Nexus: Money and Power in the Modern World 1700–2000.* London: Allen Lane.

———. 2005. "Africa Doesn't Need Handouts: It Needs Honest Governments." *The Telegraph*, March 2, 2005.

Field, E., O. Robles, and M. Torero. 2008. "The Cognitive Link Between Geography and Development: Iodine Deficiency and Schooling Attainment in Tanzania." NBER Working Paper 13838.

Filmer, D. 2004. "If You Build It, Will They Come? School Availability and School Enrollment in 21 Poor Countries." World Bank Policy Research Working Paper 3340.

Filmer, D., J. Hammer, and L. Pritchett. 2000. "Weak Links in the Chain: A Diagnosis of Health Policy in Poor Countries." *World Bank Research Observer* 15, no. 2.

Filmer, D., A. Hasan, and L. Pritchett. 2006. "A Millennium Learning Goal: Measuring Real Progress in Education." Center for Global Development Working Paper 97.

Filmer, D., and L. Pritchett. 1998. "Estimating Wealth Effects Without Expenditure Data—or Tears." World Bank Policy Research Working Paper 1994.

Filmer, D., and N. Schady. 2008. "Getting Girls into School: Evidence from a Scholarship Program in Cambodia." *Economic Development and Cultural Change* 56, no. 3.

Fink, C. 2005. "Patent Protection, Transnational Corporations and Market Structure." In C. Fink and K. Maskus, eds., *Intellectual Property and Development: Lessons from Recent Economic Research*. Washington, DC: World Bank.

Fink, C., and P. Reichenmiller. 2005. "Tightening TRIPS: The Intellectual Property Provisions of Recent US Free Trade Agreements." World Bank Trade Note No. 20.

Fisch, S. 2005. "Children's Learning from Television." *Televizion* 18.

Frech, H., and R. Miller. 1996. "The Productivity of Health Care and Pharmaceuticals: An International Comparison." UCLA Research Program in Pharmaceutical Economics and Policy, Research Paper 97, no. 1.

Freeman, J., and D. Snidal. 1982. "Diffusion, Development and Democratization: Enfranchisement in Western Europe." *Canadian Journal of Political Science* 15, no. 2.

Garrett, L. 2007. "The Challenge of Global Health." *Foreign Affairs*, January/February.

Gartner, J. 2005. *The Hypomanic Edge: The Link Between (A Little) Craziness and (A Lot of) Success in America.* New York: Simon and Schuster.

Geary, C., H. Mahler, W. Finger, and K. Shears. 2005. "Using Global Media to Reach Youth: The 2002 MTV *Staying Alive* Campaign." Family Health International Youthnet Youth Issues Paper 5, no. 1.

Gies, F., and J. Gies. 1991. *Life in a Medieval Village.* New York: Harper Perennial.

Goklany, I. 2002. "The Globalization of Human Well-Being." *Cato Policy Analysis* No. 447.

———. 2009. "Have Increases in Population, Affluence and Technology Worsened Human and Environmental Well-Being?" *The Electronic Journal of Sustainable Development* 1, no. 3.

Grenato, J., R. Inglehart, and D. Leblang. 1996. "Cultural Values, Stable Democracy, and Economic Development: A Reply." *American Journal of Political Science* 40, no. 3.

Gupta, S., B. Clements, A. Pivovarsky, and E. Tiongson. 2003. "Foreign Aid and Revenue Response: Does the Composition of Aid Matter?" IMF Working Paper, August 8.

Hazra, A., D. Bera, S. Mazumdar, and P. Datta. 2006. "Economic Inequality in Preventive Maternal and Child Health Care: A Study of Rural India." Paper presented at the WIDER Conference on Advancing Health Equity, Helsinki, Finland, September 29–30.

Heilbroner, R. 1963. *The Great Ascent: The Struggle for Economic Development in Our Time.* New York: Harper and Row.

Heinemann, A., and D. Verner. 2006. "Crime and Violence in Development: A Literature Review of Latin America and the Caribbean." World Bank Policy Research Working Paper 4041.

Hirschman, A. 1977. *The Passions and the Interests: Political Arguments For Capitalism Before Its Triumph.* Princeton, NJ: Princeton University Press.

Holla, A., and M. Kremer. 2008. "Pricing and Access: Lessons from Randomized Evaluations in Education and Health." In W. Easterly, ed., *What Works in Development? Thinking Big and Thinking Small.* Washington, DC: Brookings.

Holmes, R. 2008. *The Age of Wonder* London: Harper Press.

Human Security Centre. 2005. *Human Security Report.* University of British Columbia, Canada.

Ingram, G. 1994. "Social Indicators and Productivity Convergence in Developing Countries." In W. Baumol, R. Nelson, and E. Wolff, eds., *Convergence of Productivity: Cross-National Studies and Historical Evidence.* Oxford and New York: Oxford University Press.

Jayachandran, S., and I. Kuziemko. 2009. "Why Do Mothers Breastfeed Girls Less Than Boys?" Evidence and Implications for Child Health in India, NBER Working Paper 15041.

Jenkins, M., and B. Scott. 2007. "Behavioral Indicators of Household Decision-Making and Demand for Sanitation and Potential Gains from Social Marketing in Ghana." *Social Science and Medicine* 64.

Jensen, R., and E. Oster. 2007. "The Power of TV: Cable Television and Women's Status in India." NBER Working Paper 13305.

Jones, G., R. Steketee, R. Black, and the Bellagio Child Survival Study Group. 2003. "How Many Child Deaths Can We Prevent This Year?" *The Lancet* 362.

Kabeer, N. 2006. "Social Exclusion and the MDGs: The Challenge of 'Durable Inequalities' in the Asian Context." Paper presented at the Asia 2015 Conference, March, Overseas Development Institute, London.

Kaplan, R. 1996. *The Ends of the Earth: A Journey at the Dawn of the Twenty-First Century.* New York: Random House.

Kar, K. 2003. "Subsidy or Self-Respect? Participatory Total Community Sanitation in Bangladesh." IDS Working Paper 184.

Kaufmann, D., A. Kraay, and M. Mastruzzi. 2003. "Governance Matters III: Governance Indicators for 1996–2002." World Bank Policy Research Working Paper 3106.

Keith, L. 2002. "Constitutional Provisions for Individual Human Rights 1977–1996: Are They More Than Mere 'Window Dressing'?" *Political Research Quarterly* 55, p. N1.

Kenny, C. 1999. "Why Aren't Countries Rich? Weak States and Bad Neighborhoods." *Journal of Development Studies* 35, no. 5.

———. 2005a. "Why Are We So Worried About Income? Everything Else That Matters Is Converging." *World Development* 31, no. 1.

———. 2005b. "Does Development Make You Happy? Subjective Wellbeing and Economic Growth in Developing Countries." *Social Indicators Research* 73, no. 2.

———. 2006. *Overselling the Web? Development and the Internet.* Boulder, CO: Lynne Rienner.

———. 2007. "A Note on the Ethical Implications of the Stern Review." *Journal of Environment and Development* 16, no. 4.

———. 2008a. "The Global Expansion of Democracy and Rights: A Discussion." Available online at www.charleskenny.blogs.com.

———. 2008b. "There's More to Life than Money: Exploring the Levels/Growth Paradox in Income and Health." *Journal of International Development* 20.

————. 2008c. "What's Not Converging? East Asia's Relative Performance in Income, Health, and Education." *Asian Economic Policy Review* 3, no. 1.

————. 2008d. "What Is Effective Aid? How Would Donors Allocate
It?" *European Journal of Development Research* 20, no. 2.

————. 2008e. "The Global Expansion of Primary Education." Available online at www.charleskenny.blogs.com.

————. 2010. "Is Anywhere Stuck in a Malthusian Trap?" *Kyklos* 63.

Kenny, C., and U. Casabonne. 2008. "The Best Things in Life Are
Nearly Free: Technology, Ideas and the Global Quality of Life."
Mimeo, Center for Global Development.

Kenny, A., and C. Kenny. 2006. *Life, Liberty and the Pursuit of Utility: Happiness in Philosophical and Economic Thought.* London:
Imprint Academic.

Kenny, C., and R. Keremane. 2007. "Toward Universal Telephone
Access: Market Progress and Progress Beyond the Market."
Telecommunications Policy 31.

Kenny, C., and D. Williams. 2001. "What Do We Know About Economic Growth? Or, Why Don't We Know Very Much?" *World
Development* 29, no. 1.

Keynes, J. 1933. *Essays in Biography.* London: MacMillan.

Kiessling, J. 2007. "Democratization and Child Mortality." Stockholm
University Department of Economics Research Paper 2007:8.

Kijima, Y. 2006. "Caste and Tribe Inequality: Evidence from India,
1983–1999." *Economic Development and Cultural Change* 54,
no. 2.

Knack, S., and A. Rahman. 2004. "Donor Fragmentation and Bu-
reaucratic Quality in Aid Recipients." World Bank Policy Research Working Paper 3186.

Komlos, J. 1994. Preface. In J. Komlos, ed., *Stature, Living Standards and Economic Development.* Chicago: University of
Chicago Press.

Kothari, B., T. Bandyopadhyay, and D. Bhattacharjee. 2008. "Same-
Language Subtitling on TV: Impact on Basic Reading Develop-
ment Among Children and Adults." Mimeo, Indian Institute of
Management, Ahmedabad.

Kremer, M., and E. Miguel. 2004. "Worms: Identifying Impacts on Education and Health in the Presence of Treatment Externalities." *Econometrica* 72, no. 1.

————. 2007. "The Illusion of Sustainability." *Quarterly Journal of Economics*, August.

Kremer, M., E. Miguel, and R. Thornton. 2004. "Incentives to Learn." Harvard CID Working Paper 109.

Kristoff, N. 2008. "Birth Control for Others." *New York Times Book Review*, March 23.

Krueger, A., and J. Maleckova. 2003. "Education, Poverty and Terrorism: Is There a Causal Connection?" *The Journal of Economic Perspectives* 17, no. 4.

La Ferrara, E., A. Chong, and S. Duryea. 2008. "Soap Operas and Fertility: Evidence from Brazil." CEPR Discussion Paper 6785.

Lalumandier, J., and L. Ayers. 2000. "Fluoride and Bacterial Content of Bottled Water vs. Tap Water." *Archives of Family Medicine* 9, no. 3.

Leipziger, D. 2008. "Millennium Development Goals and Africa: An Alternative View." World Bank PREM Notes No. 116.

Levine, R. 2007. *Case Studies in Global Health: Millions Saved.* Boston: Jones and Bartlett.

Levine, R., O. Barder, and M. Kremer. 2005. *Making Markets for Vaccines: Ideas to Action.* Washington, DC: Center for Global Development.

Levine, R., and D. Renelt. 1992. "A Sensitivity Analysis of Cross-Country Growth Regressions." *American Economic Review* 82, no. 4.

Lindeboom, M, F. Portrait, and G. van den Berg. 2003. "Individual Mortality and Macro-Economic Conditions from Birth to Death." Tinbergen Institute Discussion Paper TI 2003–072/3.

Ling, J., B. Franklin, J. Lindsteadt, and S. Gearon. 1992. "Social Marketing: Its Place in Public Health." *Annual Review of Public Health* 13.

Lipset, S. M. 1959. "Some Social Requisites of Democracy: Economic Development and Political Legitimacy." *American Political Science Review* 53.

Liu, Y., W. Hsiao, and K. Eggleston. 1999. "Equity in Health and Health Care: The Chinese Experience." *Social Science and Medicine* 49.

Loevinsohn, B., and A. Harding. 2005. "Buying Results? Contracting for Health Service Delivery in Developing Countries." *The Lancet* 366.

Luby, S., M. Agboatwalla, D. Feikin, J. Painter, W. Billhimer, A. Altaf, and R. Hoekstra. 2004. "Effect of Handwashing on Child Health: A Randomised Controlled Trial." *The Lancet* 366, no. 9481.

Maddison, A. 2001. *The World Economy: A Millennial Perspective.* Paris: OECD.

Madon, G. 2003. "Energy, Poverty and Gender: Impacts of Rural Electrification on Poverty and Gender in Indonesia." Mimeo, World Bank.

McGillivray, M. 2005. "Is Aid Effective?" Paper presented at the Foundation for Development Co-operation "Financing Development Colloquium," held in Surfers Paradise, Australia, August 2004.

McNeil, M., and V. E. Letschert. 2005. "Forecasting Electricity Demand in Developing Countries: A Study of Household Income and Appliance Ownership." Proceedings of the ECEEE Summer Study 2005, Mandelieu, France. Editor: European Council for an Energy Efficient Economy.

Miguel, E., and G. Roland. 2006. "The Long-Run Impact of Bombing Vietnam." NBER Working Paper No. 11954.

Milanovic, B. 2002. "True World Income Distribution, 1988 and 1993: First Calculation Based on Household Surveys Alone." *The Economic Journal* 112, no. 476.

———. 2005. "The Modern World: The Effect of Democracy, Colonialism and War on Economic Growth 1820–2000." Mimeo, Carnegie Endowment.

———. 2008. "An Even Higher Global Inequality Than Previously Thought: A Note on Global Inequality Calculations Using the 2005 International Comparison Program Results." *International Journal of Health Services* 38, no. 3.

Moradi, A. 2006. "Nutritional Status and Economic Development in Sub-Saharan Africa, 1950–1980." Global Poverty Research Group Working Paper WPS-046.

Morrisson, C., and F. Murtin. 2005. "The World Distribution of Human Capital, Life Expectancy and Income: A Multidimensional Approach." Mimeo, London School of Economics.

———. 2009. "The Century of Education." CEP Discussion Paper 934.

Moyo, D. 2009. *Dead Aid: Why Aid Is Not Working and How There Is a Better Way for Africa*. New York: Farrar, Straus and Giroux.

Mueller, J. 2007. "The Demise of War and Speculations About the Causes Thereof." Presentation at the National Convention of the International Studies Association, Chicago, Illinois, February 26–March 4.

Narayan, D., with R. Patel, K. Schafft, A. Rademacher, and S. Koch-Schulte. 2000. *Voices of the Poor: Can Anyone Hear Us?* New York: Oxford University Press.

Nunn, N. 2008. "The Long-Term Effect of Africa's Slave Trades." *Quarterly Journal of Economics* 123, no. 1.

Olken, B. 2007. "Do Television and Radio Destroy Social Capital? Evidence from Indonesian Villages." NBER Working Paper 12561.

Osili, U. O., and B. Long. 2007. "Does Female Schooling Reduce Fertility? Evidence from Nigeria." NBER Working Paper 13070.

Oster, E. 2005. "Sexually Transmitted Infections, Sexual Behavior and the HIV/AIDS Epidemic." *Quarterly Journal of Economics* 120, no. 2.

Pasteur, K. 2005. "Community-Led Total Sanitation as a Livelihoods Entry Point: A Brief Introduction." Mimeo, IDS.

Pereira, A. 2006. "When Did Modern Economic Growth Really Start? The Empirics of Malthus to Solow." Mimeo, University of British Columbia.

Perkins, A., and M. Perkins. 1999. "Eyes Wide Shut." *Financial Planning*, December 1.

Pinker, S. 2002. *The Blank Slate: The Modern Denial of Human Nature*. London: Allen Lane.

———. 2007. "A History of Violence." *The New Republic*, March 3.

———. 2009. "Why Is There Peace?" *Greater Good*, April.

Ponting, C. 2007. *A New Green History of the World*. London: Vintage Originals.

Preston, S. 1975. "The Changing Relation Between Mortality and Level of Economic Development." *Population Studies* 29, no. 2.

Pritchett, L. 1996. "Where Has All the Education Gone?" World Bank Policy Research Working Paper 1581.

———. 1997. "Divergence Big Time." *Journal of Economic Perspectives* 11.

———. 2006. *Let Their People Come*. Washington, DC: Brookings.

Pritchett, L., and L. Summers. 1996. "Wealthier Is Healthier." *Journal of Human Resources* 31, no. 4.

Putnam, R., with R. Leonardi and R. Nanetti. 1993. *Making Democracy Work: Civic Traditions in Modern Italy*. Princeton, NJ: Princeton University Press.

Rajan, R. 2006. "Competitive Rent Preservation, Reform Paralysis, and the Persistence of Underdevelopment." NBER Working Paper 12093.

Rajan, R., and A. Subramanian. 2005. "What Undermines Aid's Impact on Growth?" IMF Working Paper WP/05/126.

Rajivan, A. 1999. "Policy Implications for Gender Equity: The India Time Use Survey, 1998–1999." International Seminar on Time Use Surveys, December 7–10, Ahmedabad.

Ranis, G., and F. Stewart. 2001. "Growth and Human Development: Comparative Latin American Experience." *The Developing Economies* 39, no. 4.

Ravallion, M. 1997. "Good and Bad Growth: The Human Development Reports." *World Development* 25, no. 5, pp. 631–638.

Ravindra, A. 2004. "An Assessment of the Impact of Bangalore Citizen Report Cards on the Performance of Public Agencies." World Bank Operations Evaluation Department Evaluation Capacity Development Working Paper No. 12.

Rees, S., R. van de Pas, D. Silove, and M. Kareth. 2008. "Health and Human Security in West Papua." *Medical Journal of Australia* 189, nos. 11–12.

Regalia, F., and L. Castro. 2007. "Performance-Based Incentives for Health: Demand- and Supply-Side Incentives in the Nicaragua

Red de Proteccion Social." Center for Global Development Working Paper 119.

Reller, M., and colleagues. 2003. "A Randomized Controlled Trial of Household-Based Flocculant-Disinfectant Drinking Water Treatment for Diarrhea Prevention in Rural Guatemala." *American Journal of Tropical Medicine and Hygiene* 69, no. 4.

Riley, J. 2001. *Rising Life Expectancy: A Global History*. Cambridge: Cambridge University Press.

Rodríguez, F. 2006. "Cleaning Up the Kitchen Sink: On the Consequences of the Linearity Assumption for Cross-Country Growth Empirics." Wesleyan University Department of Economics Working Paper 2006–4.

Ruttan, V. 2002. "Productivity Growth in World Agriculture: Sources and Constraints." *Journal of Economic Perspectives* 16, no. 4.

Sachs, J. 1996. "Growth in Africa: It Can Be Done." *The Economist,* June 29.

———. 1997. "The Limits of Convergence." *The Economist,* June 14.

———. 2005. "The End of Poverty." *Time,* March 14, 2005.

Sadique, M., and M. Asadullah. 2006. "Identifying the Effect of Public Health Programs on Child Immunisation in Rural Bangladesh." Mimeo, City University, London. Paper presented at the 2005 UKFIET Conference, Oxford, UK.

Sala-i-Martin, X. 2002. "The Disturbing 'Rise' of Global Income Inequality." NBER Working Paper 8904.

Schaffer, L. 2004. "Economic Growth and Civil War: A One-Way Street?" Paper presented at the Fifth Pan-European International Relations Conference in The Hague, Netherlands, September 9–11.

Seabright, P. 1997. "The Effect of Inequality on Collective Action." Mimeo, World Bank.

Sen, A. 1999. *Development as Freedom*. New York: Anchor Books.

Singer, P. 2002. *One World: The Ethics of Globalization*. New Haven: Yale University Press.

Soares, R. 2007. "On the Determinants of Mortality Reductions in the Developing World." NBER Working Paper 12837.

Spolare, E., and R. Wacziarg. 2006. "The Diffusion of Development." NBER Working Paper No. 12153.

Thorbecke, E., and C. Charumilind. 2002. "Economic Inequality and Its Socioeconomic Impact." *World Development* 30, no. 9.

Tooley, J. 2005. "Is Private Education Good for the Poor?" Working Paper, University of Newcastle Upon Tyne.

UN and World Bank. 2007. *Crime, Violence and Development: Trends, Costs and Policy Options in the Caribbean.* Washington, DC: World Bank.

UN Development Project. 2005. *Investing in Development: A Practical Plan to Achieve the Millennium Development Goals.* New York: United Nations.

United Nations. 2007. *The Millennium Development Goals Report.* New York: United Nations.

Vollmer, S., and M. Ziegler. 2009. "Political Institutions and Human Development: Does Democracy Fulfill its 'Constructive' and 'Instrumental' Role?" World Bank Policy Research Working Paper 4818.

Weil, D. 2005. "Accounting for the Effect of Health on Economic Growth." NBER Working Paper 11455.

World Bank. 2004. *World Development Report.* Washington, DC: World Bank.

———. 2005. *World Development Indicators.* Washington, DC: World Bank.

———. 2006. *World Development Report: Equity and Development.* New York: Oxford University Press.

———. 2007. *World Development Indicators.* Washington, DC: World Bank.

———. 2008a. *World Development Indicators.* Washington, DC: World Bank.

———. 2008b. "Rising Food Prices: Policy Options and World Bank Response." Mimeo, World Bank.

———. 2008c. *World Development Report: Reshaping Economic Geography.* Washington, DC: World Bank.

———. 2009. *World Development Indicators.* Washington, DC: World Bank.

Younger, S. 2001. "Cross-Country Determinants of Declines in Infant Mortality: A Growth Regression Approach." Mimeo, Cornell University Food and Nutrition Program."

INDEX

235